DI133879

## 'ARE YOU BLACK?

Congratulations! Ya picked up the right side of this book. It's probably the funniest half. But, be white about it, give the other half a break . . . They can be funny too. Like, it doesn't hurt the gray matter to look at life in basic black *and* white. Right?

# THE OFFICIAL BLACK FOLKS JOKE BOOK

## by Larry Wilde

PINNACLE BOOKS • NEW YORK CITY

*In memory of Aunt Bella!*
*—who lived 86 years with love*
*in her heart for everyone*

THE OFFICIAL WHITE FOLKS/BLACK FOLKS JOKE BOOK

Text copyright © 1975 by Larry Wilde

Illustrations copyright © 1975 by Bill Wenzel

An original Pinnacle Books edition, published for the first time anywhere.

ISBN: 0-523-00722-1

First printing, October 1975

*Printed in the United States of America*

PINNACLE BOOKS, INC.
275 Madison Avenue
New York, N. Y. 10016

# ABOUT THE AUTHOR

Larry Wilde, the author of three best-selling collections of ethnic and minority humor, is especially qualified to write this fourth *Official Joke Book*. Mr. Wilde is white and he grew up in a black neighborhood. In fact, he attended P.S. 14 in Jersey City, New Jersey, the same grammar school as funnyman Flip Wilson.

Larry Wilde has entertained at America's leading hotels and nightclubs and, in addition, is frequently seen on the television talk shows, in commercials and on many of the situation comedy series.

The author served two years in the United States Marine Corps and has a bachelor's degree from the University of Miami, Florida. His writing credits include articles for professional journals as well as *Genesis*, *TV Guide*, *Penthouse*, *Coronet*, and other popular magazines. He is married and lives in Los Angeles, where, between Las Vegas engagements, concert appearances, and university lectures, he conducts a class in comedy at UCLA.

# THE OFFICIAL BLACK FOLKS JOKE BOOK

# INTRODUCTION

Blacks have a unique distinction in the pages of history. No other group has suffered as much continuous and undeserved misery mainly because of the color of their skin. (Anti-Semitism has existed for over two thousand years but bigotry against Jews has been predicated on a religious and cultural difference.)

Yet Blacks, like Jews, have developed an instinctive sense of humor, rooted in their ability to laugh at the pain of poverty and prejudice. This is a good example:

*It was the first day of school. As Miss Krakower called the roll each pupil confirmed his presence. When she announced, "Hy-*

mie Greenberg," a black child raised his hand.

The teacher looked amazed. "Are you Hymie Greenberg?"

"Yes, ma'am," answered the youngster politely.

"Are you Jewish, Hymie?"

"No, ma'am," he replied. "Ain't I got enough trouble just being colored!?"

Blacks have learned to joke about adversity and quip in the face of humiliation. They have been forced to do so simply to outlast the bigots. Psychiatrists contend that only a group that can laugh at caricature and satire can survive the utter madness of man's inhumanity to man.

Much of the credit for making white America aware of the black man's sense of humor goes to Dick Gregory. Long before Gregory came upon the scene there were other Negro comics, such as Dusty Fletcher, Pigmeat Markham, and Moms Mabley, but by and large they played mostly to black audiences.

Dick Gregory pioneered the plunge into nightclubs which up to that time featured only white comedians. Suddenly, Caucasian crowds were being treated to comedy from a black point of view. They now heard about black problems and how Blacks coped with the so-called American Way of Life.

Here's a sample of Gregory's incisive social comment:

> *There's no difference between the North and the South. In the South they don't care how close I get as long as I don't get too big and in the North they don't care how big I get as long as I don't get too close.*

Blacks had always laughed at white idiosyncracies. But now there was a platform. No longer did black comics poke fun at white narrowmindedness and hypocrisy just in front of Negro audiences. The changing times brought a new freedom of comedic expression. Witness another sample of the Gregory wit:

> *When I left St. Louis I was making $5 a night. Now I'm getting $5,000 a week—for saying things out loud that I used to say under my breath.*

Laughter not only helps make life bearable for the oppressed, it also eases their relations with the oppressor. An uncensored sense of humor is the ultimate defense against a hostile society. Here's a gag that black comedians have used with great success to point up the new black attitude:

> *Two Harlemites meet. One has a bad speech impediment. "Hey, baby," asked the first Negro, "where you been?"*
>
> *"I jjjjust went ddddown to the rrrradio station to aaaudition as an aaaannouncer!" explained the stutterer.*
>
> *"Did you get the job?"*
>
> *"NNNNo, they ddddon't hire NNNNNNegroes!"*

Though for years the Negro has been the object of ridicule, the butt of white comedy, the tables now are turning. In the following pages you will find the wit and whimsy, the jocularity and jests that show the black man as he really is: Proud, religious, sensitive, athletically skilled, musically gifted, fashion conscious, education oriented, and, most of all, driven by the need to be accepted as a human being.

> So if you dig those heavy vibes
> And like to jive on juicy jibes
> Start reading and forget your sins
> You're gonna get some groovy grins.

LARRY WILDE
September 1975

4

# WE SHALL OVERCOME

The most important fight for freedom in the United States, other than this country's battle with England for independence, was the black man's struggle for civil rights. Out of that conflict came much heartbreak and tragedy—and comedy as well. Despite the riots, arrests, and unrest, America's Blacks managed to smile. Here are some of the classic lines that helped turn tears to laughter:

Two black men met on the street:

"Wasn't it awful," said the first, "how that completely unplanned, spontaneous riot started the other night?"

"Shhh," whispered the second man, "it's not till tomorrow night!"

5

"I won't say demonstrations haven't changed my life-style a little," confided a veteran civil-rights worker to a white friend. "Some of you people have a sleep-in maid. We have a sleep-in bail bondsman."

\*     \*     \*

One night, at the height of the freedom movement, a divinity student was awakened by a voice from Heaven. "Go to Mississippi! Go to Mississippi!" commanded the voice.

"All by myself?" asked the frightened student.

"Have no fear," reassured the voice, "I'll be with you—as far as Memphis!"

\*     \*     \*

"I'm not prejudiced," said a Negro to another black man. "I have lots of white friends and I treat them just like I would people."

\*     \*     \*

At the height of the riot season, Flip Wilson flipped out audiences with this filet of fun:

"I got this suit in Cleveland. Right

out of the window . . . the window was open. I don't know who threw the brick, but the window was open!"

\* \* \*

During a race riot in Detroit, the police stopped a black man driving an automobile which had a white pillowcase flying from the radio antenna.

"What's that for?" asked a patrolman.

"It's a white pillowcase," explained the driver, "to show that I'm neutral!"

The policeman quickly frisked him and discovered a pistol in his pocket.

"Neutral, eh?" said the cop. "Then what's this gun for?"

"In case somebody don't believe it," said the driver.

\* \* \*

Shortly after the Watts riot in Los Angeles, a seventeen-year-old Negro male walked into a luncheonette and ordered a cup of coffee.

"That'll be ten cents!" said the counterman.

"Sorry," said the teenager in mock innocence, "don't you know we're not paying for anything this week?!"

Before *Sanford & Son* catapulted him into the national spotlight, Redd Foxx appeared in nightclubs for many years. Redd used to get screams when he told this beauty:

"I was in Watts when the riots started. Maybe you saw my cousin on TV with the couch on his head.

" 'Are you a looter?' asked a cop.

" 'No, baby,' said my cousin. 'I'm a psychiatrist making a house call.' "

Dick Gregory eased the hardship of integration with satire:

"You should have been with me when I moved into that all-white neighborhood. You know who showed up that first day on my porch? The Negro delegation. This one Negro, Dr. Jones, he says, 'You gotta be careful in this neighborhood and cool it 'cause they're watching us.'

"I said, 'What are you all doing, stealing something?'

"He said, 'No, you know what we mean. They're goin' to look for you to depreciate some property.'

"I said, 'Buddy, they just charged me $75,000 for a $12,000 house. I'll depreciate this whole block if you let me.'

"And then Dr. Jones says, 'You act like you're goin' to be difficult. You know what we're talking about. What we're trying to say is, keep your lawn mowed and plant something out.'

"I planted watermelon, cucumbers, turnip greens, cabbage, spinach, sweet potatoes. And when them watermelons started growing my colored neighbors quit talking to me. The white folks came by every day. 'Hello, Mr. Gregory, can we have a melon?' 'Go ahead, take one!' "

# OVERHEARD AT A SELMA SIT-IN

*"Sheriff, why do you want to waste tear gas on us? We got enough to cry about already."*

\*     \*     \*

When the Senate was debating the Civil Rights Bill, one Southern Senator could not contain his concern. "Gentlemen," he shouted, "Ah believe in segregated integration, *not* integrated segregation."

\*     \*     \*

During the "separate but equal" school integration disagreement in the South, Edward R. Murrow interviewed a poor sharecropper at his humble shack in Montgomery.

"I understand," said Murrow, "that you are sending you son through college."

"That's right!"

"How do you feel about the Southern attitude toward schooling—separate but equal?"

"Well, I tell you now. They's givin' us plenty of separate but not enough equal!"

The day after a black family moved into the neighborhood, their son Richie approached Sammy, a Jewish boy, who lived nearby. "We's as good as you are," announced the young Black.

"Why is that?" asked the Jewish boy.

"You got a duplex house—we got one too!"

A week later, Richie stopped Sammy again. "We's as good as you!"

"Is that right?"

"Yeah, man! You got a Chevy Impala —we got one too!"

Another week went by, and this time Richie said to his new friend, "We's better than you!"

"Why?" asked the Jewish boy.

"We ain't got no colored people living next door to us!"

\*  \*  \*

Elvira, living in Atlanta, Georgia, who had been pregnant for eleven months, paid a visit to her obstetrician.

"I can't understand this," said the doctor after examining her. "Your baby should have been born nine weeks ago. I wonder what's holding it back."

Just then a little voice from within Elvira said, "Man, I ain't comin' out 'til I find out what school I'm goin' to."

A posse of white Mississippians trapped a black civil-rights worker on a lonely country road. Enraged, they buried him up to his neck in a sand pile and sicked a snarling dog at his exposed head.

But the black man was so skillful in dodging the dog's teeth with his head that the animal became frustrated and turned away.

Seeing what was happening, one of the tormentors spat on the man. "Nigger," he yelled. "Now stop that duckin' and dodgin' and fight my dog fair."

\* \* \*

This subtle story was circulated during the Montgomery bus strike:

A white family called in their colored cook and asked her if she supported the boycott of the buses.

"No, ma'am," said the cook. "I won't have anything to do with that affair. I plan to stay away from the buses as long as there's trouble."

\* \* \*

"What happened down there in Alabama?"

"We marched and Governor Wallace was scared and nervous. As a matter of fact, he was so scared he put Alabama in his wife's name."

Two small boys, one Indian, the other a black, got into an argument over whose race had made the greatest contribution to America.

"We got Ralph Bunche and Jackie Robinson and Mohammad Ali," said the black boy. "You Indians ain't got anybody like that to show."

"Well, we had Jim Thorpe and Geronimo," said the Indian.

"But that was a long time ago!" snapped the Black. "What have you people done to make America a better place?"

"Awright," said the Indian. "How many kids are there in America?"

"Oh, about eleventy billion, I suppose."

"How many of them you ever seen playing Cowboys and Blacks?"

\*     \*     \*

Colonel Stanford, a staunch segregationist, died and somehow made his way to Heaven. A week later, his friend Colonel Beauregard departed and was also allowed to get past the Pearly Gates.

The two of them met. "Never had any doubt we'd make it," said Colonel Beauregard, "but now that we did, tell me, how are things up here?"

14

"Not bad," answered Colonel Stanford, "but ah would advise you to watch your step. I saw God the other day, and she's a Nigrah."

*   *   *

During a one-day school boycott in Cleveland, the thousands of Negro children who participated were provided with a mimeographed "Excuse for Absence." The form had space for the child's name, the parent's signature, and carried the following explanation:

"*Reason for absence*—illness. *Nature of illness*—sick of segregation."

*   *   *

This cat was walking along the highway. A state trooper stopped him and began asking him a lot of questions. After a while, the trooper said, "Where are you from, boy?"

"I come from 'Sippi," he said.

"What do you mean—'Sippi?" said the trooper.

"I mean just what I said—'*Sippi*," he told the trooper. "Since that Supreme Court decision, I don't have to say Missis to nobody!"

"Brothers and sisters," said the minister, "my talk for today is on the subject of the status quo."

"Hold on a minute, Reverend," one of the brothers called out. "What is the status quo?"

"That," said the minister, "is the Latin name for the mess we're in."

*   *   *

And once again, Dick Gregory makes points while making us laugh:

"Last time I was down South, I walked into this restaurant and this white waitress came up to me and said, 'We don't serve colored people here!'

"I said, 'That's all right, I don't eat colored people. Bring me a whole fried chicken.'

"About that time these three cousins came in. You know the ones I mean, Klu, Kluck, and Klan. And they say, 'Boy, we're givin' you fair warnin'. Anything you do to that chicken, we're gonna do to you.'

"About then the waitress brought me my chicken. 'Remember, boy, anything you do to that chicken, we're gonna do to you.'

"So I put down my knife and fork, and I picked up that chicken and I *kissed* it."

16

## COOL, MAN, COOL

Irish irony is a brand of wit unto itself. Jewish jokes have their own special flavor. And there is a sense of humor indigenous to Blacks. It is playful, gentle, good-natured, happy, and best of all, just plain funny. Now enjoy a little Black on Black:

A man hopped in a cab at the Atlanta airport and in a short time began chatting with the driver. "What is your name, uncle?" he asked.

"Abraham Lincoln, suh!"

"That's a name familiar to everybody in this part of the country."

"I reckon, suh, it oughter be, 'cause I've been drivin' heah evah since World War Two."

17

"What dat contraption, Doctor?"

"That Sam, is a sphygmomano-meter!"

"Sho! That is what ah was afraid it was!"

*   *   *

Altie and Big Bertha stood before the altar. Big Bertha weighed 200 pounds, her groom a mere 100.

"Does you take dis woman for your lawful wedded wife?" asked the minister.

"Ah takes nothin'!" replied Altie. "Ah's bein' took."

*   *   *

Luther and James worked in a hotel. They were chatting during their coffee break.

"This morning the boss tell me I gotta show courtesy and tact to the guests," said Luther. "What's he mean by those words?"

"Well, ah'll elucidate," replied James. "Yesterday ah opens the bathroom and there was a lady in the tub. So ah says, ' 'Scuse me, suh' and departs. Now, that ' 'scuse me' was courtesy, whereas the 'suh' was tact."

Old white-haired Leonard was sitting down hollering one day. "Wassa matter with you, ol' man?" asked his wife.

"Ah'm sittin' on a nail," answered Leonard.

"Well, why don't you move?"

"Tha's awright," he replied in a tired voice. "Ah'll get used to it shortly."

* * *

"Hello! That you, Coral?"

"Yes, suh!"

"You gonna marry me?"

"Sure am, honey! Who this on the phone?"

* * *

Mose went over to Daniel's house, hoping to borrow his donkey for a few hours' work.

"Why, he ain't heah," explained Daniel. "My oldes' boy done rid him inter town."

Just then the donkey brayed loudly from his stall behind the house. Mose looked at Daniel suspiciously.

"Hey," he said, "that sho' don't sound like he's been rid inter town."

"Now, wait a minute!" shouted Daniel. "You mean you gonna take de donkey's word against mine?"

Curtis was courting Adela.

"Honey," he said, "you remind me fo' all de world of brown sugar."

"How come, Curtis?"

"You am so sweet and so unrefined."

Elijah got himself a job in a circus as a roustabout. His first assignment was to tidy up the lion's cage.

"No, suh," he protested. "Ah's not gonna go in that lion's cage to clean it out."

"There's nothing to be afraid of," said the circus manager. "That lion is old and toothless, and we feed him on milk."

"Yes, suh! Ah was toothless and they fed me on milk—but ah eats meat now!"

\* \* \*

*Roy:* You's a liar!
*Joe:* Say that again and I'll bust yo jaw.
*Roy:* Consider it said again.
*Joe:* Consider yo jaw busted!

\* \* \*

Waters walked into his savings bank and asked to withdraw three dollars.

"I'm sorry," said the teller, "but the iron rule of this institution is that you cannot withdraw less than five dollars."

"All, right," said Waters, "I'll take the five."

After receiving his money, Waters

handed back two dollars to the teller and said, "Now, suh, if you please, ah'd like to deposit two dollars in this institution."

*   *   *

"Look heah, 'Zekiel, I come 'round to your house the other day to see you 'bout that ten dollars you owe me, but you didn't come to the door when I knocked. How come?"

"Probably 'cause I wasn' home, Odum."

"Oh, yes, you were home all right."

"What makes you think so?"

"I know you was home, 'cause your shirt was hangin' on the line!"

*   *   *

"Ada, you know we're all very fond of you," said a Short Hills housewife to her cook. "I hope you like your room and are happy with your wages. I'm also thinking of giving you one of my silk slips."

"Oh, Lord, Mrs. Pressman! How many folks have you gone and asked for dinner now?"

During a break Nate and his boss were passing the time of day over coffee. "How're you and your wife getting on?" he asked.

"Oh, my wife pesters me a lot by asking me for money," replied Nate. "Ah come home at night tired to death, nothing but work, work, all the time, and she says nothing but 'Money, money, money. Give me twenty dollars, give me ten dollars, give me five dollars!'"

"What on earth does she do with all that money?"

"Ah don't know!" said Nate. "Ah ain't give her none yet!"

\* \* \*

| Housewife: | Lizzie, I notice you have been taking our empty grapefruit hulls home with you. What in the world do you do with them? |
| Lizzie: | Well, ma'am, they sure do make my garbage look stylish. |

\* \* \*

"Pass the 'lasses," said Eloise.
"Don't say 'lasses," corrected her

northern Aunt Daphne. "Say molasses."

"How can I say mo' 'lasses, when I ain't had none yet!"

*       *       *

Otis and Addie took their first Caribbean cruise. They were out at sea only two days when Addie came rushing into the cabin, where Otis had been moaning since he got aboard.

"Hey, you Otis!" she cried. "Come on out on deck. We're passing a ship!"

"A ship, huh?" said Otis. "Don't call me until we're passin' a tree!"

*       *       *

*Patient:*  Is the doctor in?
*Maid:*  No, suh!
*Patient:*  Have you any idea when he will be back?
*Maid:*  I don't know, suh. He went out on an eternity case.

*       *       *

"Ada, did the doctor find out what was troublin' you?"

"Yep! He said I was sufferin' from 'cute indiscretion."

"Suh, can I have de evening off to go to de lodge? It's important, for I's de Sublime King."

"Why, you only joined the lodge two weeks ago, and you tell me you're the Sublime King already?"

"Yessuh. You see, in our lodge, de Sublime King am de lowest office dere is."

\* \* \*

*Employer:* Ossie, did you go to your lodge meeting last night?

*Ossie:* Nossuh. We dun have to pos'pone it.

*Employer:* How is that?

*Ossie:* De Grand All-Powerful Invincible Most Supreme Unconquerable Potentate dun got beat up by his wife.

\* \* \*

John D. Rockefeller, impressed by the efficiency and attentiveness of the Pullman porter on duty in his car, called the man over near the end of the trip. "What's your average tip on a run like this?" asked the millionaire.

"Oh, about two dollars, I guess," replied the porter.

Mr. Rockefeller snapped two singles out of his wallet and handed them over. "You must do pretty well on this job," he smiled.

"Hasn't been too good lately," said the porter. "This is the first average tip I've had in months."

\*     \*     \*

Manson, sleepy-eyed and only half awake, climbed out of his upper berth and called for the porter.

"Say," he shouted, "didn't I give you five dollars to be sure and see that I got off at Cleveland?"

"For land's sake," replied the porter. "No wonder that gentleman was makin' such a fuss this mornin' when I put him off the train!"

\*     \*     \*

"Mrs. Charles, you sure have three fine little daughters," said Mrs. Giovanni, her neighbor. "What are their names?"

"De first is Emerald, de second is Pearl, and de baby is Onyx."

"Why did you ever name the child Onyx?"

" 'Cause she was onyxpected!"

*Moses:* Does this lodge yo' belong to have any death benefits?

*Levi:* Yessuh! 'Deed it does. When yo' dies, yo' don' hab to pay no more dues.

\* \* \*

Jamie came home from school one afternoon. "Say, Pop," he said, "will you help me with my 'rithmetic? The teacher says we got to find the least common denominator."

"My Gawd, ain't they found that thing yet?" yelled his father. "Why, they was looking for it when *I* was a boy."

\* \* \*

Granville had removed his shirt and was seated on the front porch searching busily for bugs on the garment.

Just then, his friend Julius passed. "Hey, man!" he said. "What you doin'?"

"Lookin' for them 'rithmetic bugs," replied Granville.

" 'Rithmetic bugs? Why do you call them that?"

" 'Cause they adds to my misery, they subtracts from my pleasure, they divides my attention, an' they multiplies like the dickens!"

Cleophus and Lionel were fishing on the side of a bank. In the course of the conversation, the subject of marriage came up.

"What do you call it when a gal gits married three times?" asked Cleophus. "Biology?"

"You suttingly is an ignoramus!" replied Lionel. "When she gits married *two* times, that's biology. When she gits married *three* times, that's trigonometry!"

\*　　\*　　\*

George walked into a swanky bar on Woodward Avenue of the Motor City and ordered a bottle of beer. He handed the black bartender a dollar bill and was shocked to receive ninety cents change. "Isn't there some mistake?" asked George.

"No," said the barkeep. "A dime is all I'm charging you."

Twenty minutes later, George ordered a ham and cheese on rye. "That'll be fifteen cents!" said the barman.

"I can't understand it!" George exclaimed. "How can you sell this stuff so cheap?"

"Look, buddy, I just work here!" said the black man. "The boss is upstairs with my wife. And what he's doin' to my wife, I'm doin' to his business!"

## BLACK IS BEAUTIFUL

An NAACP official telephoned the Library of Congress and told the chief librarian that the library had 18,000 books with the word "nigger" in them and that all the books had to be removed in a week.

"But," protested the librarian, "we have 50,000 volumes with the word 'bastard' in them."

"I know," said the official, "but those bastards aren't organized."

\*   \*   \*

Did you hear about the black boys running toward their swimming hole, shouting, "The last one in is a dirty Polack!"?

A Negro was jumping up and down on a manhole cover on a street in Detroit, shouting: "Thirty-nine! Thirty-nine! Thirty-nine!"

Along came Lowandowski. "What you do?" he asked.

"Here man," said the Black, "you jump for a while."

Lowandowski began leaping up and down on the manhole cover. Suddenly, the Black snatched the cover away and the Polack fell into the sewer.

The colored man replaced it and, jumping up and down, shouted: "Forty! Forty! Forty!"

*　　*　　*

"What would you call a six-foot-four Black with a knife in his hand?"

"Sir!"

*　　*　　*

Slappy White has Las Vegas audiences rolling in the aisles with this one:

"When the slogan *Black is beautiful* came out I really went for it. *Black is beautiful.* I bought it all the way. I painted my house black—inside and out. First thing that happened, I couldn't find my bowling ball.

"Then all of a sudden, I lost my wife and two kids."

"Are you gonna join the NAACP?"

"Not me!"

"I heard they is tryin' to help us."

"Mebbe so. But I ain't joinin'. Fella where I work says NAACP stands for Negroes Are Actually Colored Polacks."

Black folks can get a cab any time in New York. All they have to do is rent a white person and pay him five dollars an hour to do the hailing for him.

\* \* \*

Henry walked into a Chinatown tavern and said to the Oriental behind the bar, "Hey, Chink, give me a drink!"

Ten minutes later, Henry called out again, "All right, Chink, give me a drink!"

A short time passed and once again Henry shouted, "Hey, Chink, give me another drink!"

"Say," said the bartender, "I have held my temper. You come behind bar and see how you like to be insulted!"

The two men exchanged places. "Okay," said the Oriental. "Now, you nigger, give me a jigger!"

"Sorry," said Henry, "we don't serve Chinks in here!"

\* \* \*

Mrs. Kendrick walked up to the bus station window and said, "Gimme a ticket!"

"Where to?" asked the agent. "Where are you going?"

"None of your business where I'm going," she replied. "White folks wants to know too much about black folks' business. You just give me a ticket."

*   *   *

Jimmie Walker, the brilliant young comedy actor on the hit television show *Good Times*, began his career as a stand-up comedian. He still plays concert dates and clubs. Here's a bit of his blockbuster routine:

"Let's face it. I am a eb-o-ny genius. A bronzed Adonis. I have attained a new plane in blackery.

"But it wasn't always so *in* bein' black. When I was a kid, my mother used to say, 'Jimmie, you so dark—lighten up! Suck in your lips!'

"When I was in school we did a production of 'Snow White and the Seven Dwarfs.' Had to bus in Snow White.

"I heard they're gonna make a sequel to *American Graffiti*, so I went to audition for a part. They say, 'What you doin' here, man? Don't you know there were no blacks in the Fifties?' That's right. We was all standin' around waitin' for the Sixties."

Naomi hit the numbers real big and decided to buy a mink with her winnings. As she stood in front of the store mirror, the mink down to her ankles, she turned to the white saleslady and asked, "Don't you think this coat makes me look too Jewish?"

Nipsey Russell, on a Dean Martin Show "Roast" of Telly Savalas, kidded the star of *Kojak* like this:

"What does a Greek know about being a law enforcement officer? All the great detectives have been my people: Boston Blackie, Sam Spade, The Shadow!"

\*     \*     \*

Two men, one white, the other black, stood side by side on a bus. Suddenly, the white man reached out and picked something off the black man's sleeve.

"Take your hand offen me," shouted the black man. "What you doing touching me?"

"You got a bedbug on your coat."

"Put it back," said the black man. "Getting so black folks can't have nothing but what you white folks want to take it away."

\*     \*     \*

Comedy writer Bruce Howard tells about the four Blacks in a car going ninety miles an hour. The car careens out of control, crashes into a brick wall. The auto's four occupants are strewn about the ground. By some miracle none is hurt but all are still in a daze.

A policeman approached the group and shouted, "All right, who the hell was driving?"

"Nobody," said one of the men. "We was all in the back seat turnin' on!"

* * *

*Black Tennis Player* (to three white players): "Anybody for a game of mixed doubles?"

* * *

A colored maid and her white employer became pregnant at the same time and gave birth on the same day. A few months later the white woman came running into the kitchen and exclaimed to the maid:

"My baby said his first word today."

In the crib the colored baby sat up and said, "He did? What did he say?"

* * *

"I'm going to give you three days to get your rent paid up," the landlord announced to Mr. Barnes.

"Okay," said Barnes. "I'll take Christmas, Easter, and the Fourth of July."

One of joyful George Kirby's funniest jokes is about the transplant of a Black's heart into a white man:

"Not only did the white man live," says George, "he went to Harlem and won a tap dancing contest.

"When he went home, he found three welfare checks waitin' for him and the finance company drivin' his Cadillac away."

\* \* \*

A landlord called for his rent, many weeks overdue. He was naturally annoyed when his tenant explained the unhappy state of affairs.

"I's really most indeedy sorry," said the tenant, "but I just can't pay you this week."

"But you said that last week!" cried the landlord. "And the week before, and the week before."

"Well," said the tenant, "doesn't I keep my word?"

\* \* \*

SIGN IN HARLEM
HABERDASHERY

*Think Yiddish*
*Dress British*

"Landlady," said Earl, "there's a dead bedbug in my bed!"

"Go to sleep," said the landlady, "it ain't gonna hurt you."

"I ain't afraid of it," said Earl. "It's the twenty thousand coming to the funeral I'm worried about."

\* \* \*

*Buck* (Washington) and (John) *Bubbles* (Sublett) were a great comedy team in the early Thirties. Here is a sample of some material that broke up audiences all over America:

*Buck:* Boy, I sure can run.

*Bubbles:* You sure can run all right. What was you runnin' up the street for this mornin'?

*Buck:* Oh, I was just runnin' to stop a fight!

*Bubbles:* Yeah, well who was fightin'?

*Buck:* Me and another fella!

*Bubbles:* Whatcha you wanna *run* fer?

*Buck:* You cra-a-zy? You don't think my legs is gonna stand around and see my body *abused*, do ya?

*Bubbles:* Yeah, but why didn't you stay there?

*Buck:* Now there you go again. My father told me any time that I see somebody was gonna hit me—for me to leave there!

41

These cats are having themselves a little jam session. They're really wailing. Pretty soon they hear a knock on the door. One of them opens up and the owner of the building is standing there.

"I'm sorry to bust in on you like this," said the landlord, "but do you know there's a sick old lady moaning upstairs?"

"No," said the cat, "but if you give us the first few bars we can pick up on it."

Ed Coleman, the super Rancho Park, California, golf pro, tells about Billings, the typical Madison Avenue advertising executive who hopped on the evening train to Darien, Connecticut. He sat down and began to settle in for his trip home when he noticed a huge, good-looking black man sitting across the aisle.

"He'll probably get off at 125th Street in Harlem," thought Billings.

But he didn't. "There's a lot of them live in Stamford. He'll get off there!" sneered Billings as the train pulled out.

But he didn't. To make matters worse, the black man was now reading *The Wall Street Journal*. Furthermore, to Billings' even greater dismay, the black man was expensively dressed in tasteful, well-tailored clothes.

Finally, the train arrived in Darien. Billings got off and headed for his wife waiting in their Ford station wagon. Suddenly, he noticed the black man had also left the train and was now getting behind the wheel of a Rolls-Royce.

The ad exec was white with redneck rage. He rushed up to the Rolls and began banging furiously on the window. "Nigger! Nigger! Nigger!" shouted Billings.

The black man quickly rolled down the window, looked about, and said haughtily, "Where? Where?"

Mr. Johnson walked into the Internal Revenue office to discuss his tax return. Another Black behind the desk said, "What is your name?"

"Rufus Rastus Johnson!"

"That's impossible," retorted the government man. "*My* name is Rufus Rastus Johnson. How do you spell it?"

The taxpayer picked up a pencil and wrote: "X X X."

"That's the same way I spell mine," announced the tax collector. "But after that I put . . ." And he added: X X X.

"What does that mean?"

"C.P.A."

\* \* \*

"What is your name?"

"Booker T. Washington Smith."

"Can you sign your name?"

"Suh?"

"I ask can you write your name."

"No, suh! Ah never writes my name. Ah dictates it, suh!"

\* \* \*

Two junkies were watching a Polish family moving into the worst block in Harlem. "Oh, oh!" one said to the other. "There goes the neighborhood."

Why are there so few black messhall attendants aboard modern U.S. Navy vessels?

Most of them have been replaced by Polacks.

* * *

Pearson was told by the white manager of an employment agency to report to the Eagle Laundry.

"Mister, isn't there somewhere else you can send me?"

"What's wrong?" asked the manager.

"I'll do almost anything," answered Pearson. "I ain't proud and I ain't lazy, but I ain't gonna wash no eagles either."

* * *

Newhouse applied to a job at a Nashville Negro Employment Agency. They immediately took down his qualifications and put them in a computer. In a moment the machine spelled out:

BIMM HY BART PCT

"Ah," thought Newhouse, "I'm finally gonna make me some good money. BIMM is short for that famous nightclub, Bimbo's. HY is short for Hollywood. BART means I'll be a bartender.

And PCT stands for percentage of the profits."

"Now may I tell you what the computer has spelled out for you?" asked the employment director.

"I already know, but you go ahead."

"Well, the computer spelled out: BIMM HY BART PCT. And this is how it breaks down:

BIMM —*Be In Memphis Monday;*
HY —*Have Your;*
BART —*Black Ass Ready To;*
PCT —*Pick Cotton Tuesday.*"

* * *

The immortal Moms Mabley has made comic history with her hilarious tale of "Little Cindy-Ella":

"You-all call her Cinderella in that book you-all got. Anyhow, way down South lived a little girl. She had long black hair, pretty brown eyes, pretty brown skin. Well, let's face it—she was colored.

"Cindy-Ella turns to the mirror and says: 'Mirror, mirror, on the wall, who's the fairest one of all?'

"The mirror replies: 'Snow White—and don't you forget it.'"

47

# SLOGAN FOR SUPPORT NATIONAL BROTHERHOOD WEEK

*Take a chocolate goodie home tonight.*

\* \* \*

*White man:* I don't know what to do, my house has burned to the ground, my wife died, my car's been stolen, and the doctor says I gotta have a serious operation.

*Black man:* What you kickin' about, you white ain't you?

\* \* \*

Comedian Irwin C. Watson takes a gentle, self-mocking, cerebral approach to Blackness:

"I wasn't too surprised to hear there was a group starting a Back-to-Africa movement. They say that within the next ten years all of the people of African descent will be goin' back to Africa. It warmed my heart. Every time I see one of them I wish him a pleasant voyage. See, 'cause I'm not goin'. I figure with all them goin' to Africa and all the white men goin' to the moon, they'll soon just be me, some Puerto Ricans and Chinese fightin' to keep those Indians on the reservation."

Jesse and Rafael were playing down in a railroad yard. "Hey, you best get away from that railroad track!" warned Jesse. "That train'll come whizzin' by and suck you off!"

"Come on, train!" shouted Rafael. "Come on, train!"

\* \* \*

Booker T. Washington once gave a speech in a small town in Georgia. When he had finished, an old Confederate soldier, white-haired and white-mustached, pushed forward to the platform, his face aglow with enthusiasm.

"Doctor Washington," he declared, "I want to do now what I never thought I'd be doing. I want to clasp your hand and pledge you my support for the great work you are doing. And furthermore, I want to tell you this: That was the best speech I ever heard in my life and you are the greatest man in this country today!"

"I am afraid you do me too much honor," said Washington. "Wouldn't you regard Teddy Roosevelt as the greatest man we have?"

"Huh!" exploded the Southerner. "I've had no use for him since he invited you to eat a meal with him at the White House."

Paul was riding his bicycle on a blistering hot summer day. But the heat and fatigue had finally so gotten to him that he stopped and sat down beside the road. Minutes later, a small Mercedes pulled up. "Anything wrong?" asked the man behind the wheel.

"No, sir, I'm on my way to town," replied the black boy. "I'm just plumb tuckered out."

"As you can see I don't have enough room for you and your bicycle," said the occupant of the Mercedes "But if you tie your bike to my rear bumper, you can sit on it and I'll tow you!"

In a few moments, the car, pulling the black boy on his bicycle, headed down the highway. At the first stop light, a Jaguar pulled alongside. "Hey," said the man inside, "wanna race?"

"You got it!" was the reply.

They were soon racing at over 120 miles an hour, the Mercedes driver having completely forgotten about the black boy behind him on the bike.

Both cars were up to 140 when they passed a squad car. The bewildered police officer quickly picked up his radio mike. "Hey, Sarge, you ain't gonna believe this!" he shouted. "A Jaguar's racing a Mercedes all hell bent for leather and there's some white kid following them on a bicycle!"

*Policeman:* "...There's a white kid following them on a bicycle!"

"He is suffering from Dunlaps' disease."

"What is Dunlaps' disease?"

"His stomach done-laps over his belt!"

*     *     *

During the Louis-Schmelling fight, some observers felt that because Louis was knocked out, he had been slipped a "mickey."

In the dressing room, one of the reporters asked, "Joe, were you drugged?"

"Only when I was knocked down and drugged back to my corner!"

*     *     *

Joe Louis and Billy Conn appeared on the TV show *The Way It Was* and watched a replay of their world heavyweight title fight in 1941.

After it was over, Conn turned to Louis and said, "If I'd stayed away from you for three more rounds, I could have been champion of the world for six months."

"You had it for twelve rounds and couldn't keep it," answered the Brown Bomber. "How could you keep it for six months?"

Football is one of the most popular sports among black people. It's the only sport in the world in which a black man can chase a white man and 80,000 people stand up and cheer.

*     *     *

Hall-of-Famer Satchel Paige, considered to be the greatest black pitcher of all time, talked as colorfully and spiritedly as he pitched. Here are some of his classic delicacies of wit:

"Avoid fried meats, which anger up the blood.

"If your stomach disputes you, lie down and pacify it with cool thoughts.

"Keep your juices flowing by jangling around gently as you move.

"Go very light on the vices, such as carrying on in society; the social ramble ain't restful.

"Avoid running at all times.

"Don't ever look back. Something might be gaining on you."

And, of course, there is Paige's classic comment on Cool Papa Bell, dubbed the Ty Cobb of black baseball, who is also in the Hall of Fame:

"He was so fast he could turn out the light and jump into bed before the room got dark."

Erroll Garner, one of the authentic jazz pianists of our time, cannot read or write music. Nevertheless, he commands the respect of musical authorities and the enthusiasm of millions of ordinary listeners.

A critic once asked him, "How is it that you can make such wonderful music without being able to read a note?"

Garner shrugged: "A beaver don't have to go to engineering school to know how to build a dam."

*     *     *

George Shearing, the blind pianist, says Las Vegas is very frustrating for him. "I'm playing the blacks and whites and everybody else is playing the blacks and reds."

*     *     *

When Bill Cosby started out as a nightclub entertainer, his performance included a monologue in which he impersonated the first Negro President, in the White House, chatting with a friend. At one point Cosby would say: "Yeah, buddy, everything's fine (pause) . . . except there's a lot of 'For Sale' signs going up in this block."

This is another classic from Slappy White:

"One time Redd Foxx and me went down to Tijuana in Mexico and we found this cute little monkey. Well, we wanted to bring it back to Los Angeles for a pet but we were afraid the Customs Inspectors wouldn't let us.

"So we went into this ladies' shop down on the main drag, bought the monkey a little dress and a hat, put it between us in the car and drove right up to the border gate.

"The Inspector looked in the car, asked if we hadn't anything to declare, we said 'no,' so he waved us on.

"As we were pulling away, I heard one customs officer say to the other one, 'Isn't that the way it always happens! Any time you see a Mexican girl who looks halfway decent she's out with a couple of spooks!'"

\* \* \*

## HERE COME DE JUDGE

"Mr. Martin, have you ever been up before me?"

"I don't know, Your Honor! What time does you get up?"

*     *     *

*Judge:* This is a serious charge. You want me to appoint a lawyer to defend you?

*Prisoner:* Naw, suh, Judge, thank you. Every time I've had a lawyer they locks me up in the calaboose, and let the lawyer go free. This time, Judge, I'm gonna throw myself on the ignorance of the cou't.

*Papa loves Mama*
*Mama loves men.*
*Now Mama's full of buckshot*
*And Papa's in the pen.*

\*     \*     \*

*Judge:* Turner, is your wife dependent upon you?

*Turner:* She sho' is, Judge. If I didn't go out and get the washin' and bring it home for her to do, she'd starve to death.

\*     \*     \*

Virgil kept answering questions with: "Well, I think . . ."

"Don't think," interrupted the lawyer. "Tell us what you know, not what you think."

"Well, I'm not a lawyer," said Virgil. "I can't just talk without thinking."

\*     \*     \*

*Black Attorney:* Mistah Greene, I have discovered that I can get your divorce on the grounds that your marriage isn't legal. Her father didn't have a license to carry a gun.

| | |
|---|---|
| *Judge:* | Sorry, Mrs. Watkins, but I can't issue a marriage license for your daughter. She's only fifteen and that's too young. |
| *Mrs. Watkins:* | That don't help us out none, Judge. Is you trying to tell me that she's too young to do what she already done did? |

\*     \*     \*

Freeman King, the talented television comedy actor, tells about the black gentleman who was arrested for shooting a man. The next morning he was brought into court.

"Why did you shoot that man?" asked the judge.

" 'Cause he called me a black sonuvaby his wife for nonsupport.

"You didn't have any business shooting a man for that!"

"Well, now, Your Honor, what would you have done if he called you that?"

"Oh, he wouldn't have called me that!"

"I know, Judge, but suppose he'd called you the kind of a sonufabitch you is?"

Bernardette showed up at work after spending the morning in court. "Did you get your divorce?" asked Mrs. Smith, her employer.

"Yes, ma'am!" replied Bernadette.

"Did you get any alimony from your husband?"

"No, Mrs. Smith, but he done give me a first class reference."

\*　　\*　　\*

Judge:　And furthermore, Mr. Mitchell, I'm going to award your wife a divorce, and I'm going to give her thirty dollars a week alimony.

Mitchell:　That's right nice of you, Your Honor. I'll try to slip her a couple of bucks myself from time to time.

\*　　\*　　\*

Oletha came out of the courtroom sobbing uncontrollably. A kindly attendant asked her what the trouble was.

"My husband jest divorced me," she cried, "and the judge give him custody of all three of the chillun. Now, is that fair? 'Specially since none of them was his kids anyhow!"

TV Director Stan Zabka tells about

Sarah and Malcolm standing before the judge to be married.

"This license is not filled out properly," boomed the magistrate. "Take it back downstairs to the clerk."

Sarah and Malcolm trudged down the four flights of stairs and now once again were in the judge's chambers. "I can't marry you," exclaimed his Honor. "The clerk forgot to sign it."

Again Sarah and Malcolm staggered down and then back up the four flights of stairs. "All right," said the judge, "let me see. This marriage license still isn't filled out properly. You take it back down to the clerk and have him do it all over again!"

The weary couple once more made the four-flight trip. "Now," said the judge, looking over the marriage license, "I think we can proceed." Suddenly, he noticed a little boy hanging onto the woman's skirt.

"Who's that child?" thundered the judge.

"He belongs to us," murmured Malcolm.

"I suppose you realize that in the eyes of the law he's a bastard!"

"That's funny," said Malcolm. "The man downstairs said you was!"

*Judge:* Alvin, I cannot conceive of a meaner, more cowardly act than yours of running away from your wife. Do you realize you are a deserter?

*Alvin:* If you knowed that lady as I does, you wouldn't be calling me no deserter. Ah is a refugee—that's what ah is!

        \*       \*       \*

*Thelma:* I wants a divorce from that husband of mine.

*Judge:* When were you married?

*Thelma:* Three days ago!

*Judge:* Married only three days and you want a divorce?

*Thelma:* Yes, sir! That man is too much! He just won't let me get any sleep.

*Judge:* I see, then, you want to file your application, is that it?

*Thelma:* File my application? Lawd, no! I can't even touch it with a powder puff!

        \*       \*       \*

*Magistrate:* Well, Josh, I see you're back for fighting with your wife. Liquor again?

*Josh:* No suh! Judge, this time she licked me!

The judge had just passed sentence on Cleon. It was Cleon's third conviction for chicken stealing, and as he stood in court, he was heard to mutter something heavily to himself.

"What's that you said?" demanded the judge. "It sounded like profanity."

"Ah didn't say nuthin', suh," said Cleon.

"Yes, you did," insisted his Honor, "and I want you to repeat it out loud."

"Well, suh," said Cleon, "all I said was, 'God am de judge,' suh, 'God am de judge.'"

*       *       *

Los Angeles lawyer Alan Saltzman listened in on this lollapalooza:

"And tell the court *exactly*," demanded the attorney, "how far the car was from the fire hydrant on the northeast corner of La Brea and Olympic Boulevard."

"The car," offered Newcombe, "was exactly 15 yards, 10 feet, 11¾ inches from the hydrant."

"How can the witness be so specific in his reply?" asked the attorney.

"I figured that some idiot lawyer would demand to know the exact distance—so I measured it."

Judge to defendant: "Colonel Willis, why are you called 'Colonel'? I don't think you were ever in the army. What regiment were you in?"

"Well, suh, it's like this. The 'Colonel' in front of my name is like when someone calls you the 'Honorable' Judge Morton. It don't mean a thing!"

\* \* \*

Judge:      You again! On another drunk charge! Hampton, didn't I tell you I didn't want to see you here again?

Hampton:    Yes, suh! Dat's what I tried to tell these policemen, but they wouldn't believe me.

\* \* \*

A Negro had been called as a witness in the trial of a friend who was charged with stealing.

"How long have you known the accused?" asked the prosecutor.

"Jus' about ten yeahs."

"And would you consider him to be a thief?"

"Well, ah wouldn't 'xactly considah he was a thief, suh. But if ah was a chicken, ah'd sho' roost high!"

Jeeter had been charged with stealing a Smithfield ham, so he hired a lawyer.

"If you are innocent, we ought to be able to prove an alibi," said the shyster attorney. "Have you got one? About what time was the ham stolen?"

"Dey say it wuz tuck about eleven o'clock."

"Well, where were you between ten o'clock and midnight—in bed, shall we say?"

"Oh, no, suh. I had to hide de ham fust."

\* \* \*

"Your wife here has testified that you beat her. Is that right?"

"Well, I hit her once with an oak leaf."

"An oak leaf. That doesn't sound so bad."

"Your honor," interrupted the wife, "it was an oak leaf from the dining room table."

\* \* \*

*Judge:* That'll be twenty dollars or twenty days.

*Jones:* I'll take the twenty dollars.

Elderly Mosely, driving an elderly automobile, was arrested for ignoring a red traffic light. When he was brought to court, the judge asked him if he had any explanation to make.

"I didn't mean no harm, Y'Honor," said the old man.

"Then why did you do it?" the judge asked.

"Well, when I saw all those white folks driving through the green light, I just natcherally thought the red light was for colored."

\*  \*  \*

Armstrong was brought into court for nonsupport by his wife.

"Young man," said the judge, "your wife says you have twelve children and you don't support them. How can a man who doesn't support his family want to have so many children?"

"Your Honor," said Armstrong, "when I get that feelin', I feel I could support the whole world!"

\*  \*  \*

*Prosecutor:* Can you tell me if the defendant was expensively garbed?

*Lucius:* Deed she was, suh! Ah knows 'spensive garbage when ah sees it.

"So, it's a deal. You can be my lawyer, and I'll give you a hundred to do my worrying for me."

"It's a deal. Where's the hundred?"

"That's your first worry!"

*       *       *

Gilliam was seated in the witness stand. He had already calmly answered all the questions of the prosecuting attorney. Now it was the judge's turn.

"Does the defendant really expect this court of law to accept his story that the completely assembled still on his property was not being used for the purpose of producing illicit whiskey?"

"That's right, Your Honor!" said Gilliam. "I bought that as a novelty, a conversation piece. I do not now, nor have I ever, operated it as a still to produce whiskey."

"Hogwash!" howled the magistrate. "As far as this court is concerned, possession of the equipment is proof enough of your guilt!"

"Then, Your Honor, I guess you'd also better charge me with raping your daughter!"

"What!" screamed the judge. "Did you rape my daughter?"

"No, sir," said Gilliam. "But she was at my place last night and I sure got the equipment for it!"

Stukes reported for jury duty and then asked to be excused because he was prejudiced.

"I took one look at those shifty eyes, Your Honor," said Stukes, "and I knew right away he was just as guilty as sin."

"Sit down," snapped the judge. "That's the lawyer!"

*     *     *

Althea was a generous young woman, so when her boyfriend got into trouble she offered to act as a character witness. Althea sat on the stand very calmly despite the prosecuting attorney's sizzling cross-examination.

"You say that you are sufficiently well acquainted with the defendant to know that he would never steal?"

"Dat's right, suh."

"Are you positive that he would never steal, even if he were in desperate need of funds?"

"Ah certainly thinks so, suh!"

"Do you yourself know what it means to be in dire need of money? Have you ever been financially embarrassed?"

"Well," answered Althea, "you might say dat ah has often been pushed fo' money."

*     *     *

## JUMPIN' AND JIVIN'

Rafe finally convinced his white chick, Martha, to go to a motel with him. As they prepared for bed, Martha needed further assurance.

"Rafe, dear," she cooed softly, "will you love me always?"

"Sure, baby," he murmured, "which way do you want me to try first?"

\*     \*     \*

"How you makin' out with that good-lookin' blonde airline hostess?"

"Real good!" replied Raymond. "Tonight I'm plannin' to play 'Road Builder' with her!"

"What the heck is 'Road Builder'?"

"I talk her into laying down and then I black top her!"

"Jackson, what was the time you was the most scared in your whole life?"

"That's easy. It was the time 'Razor' Brown came home and found me on the couch with his wife."

"What makes you so sure that was your worst scare?"

" 'Cause, Brown, he took one look at me and said to his wife, 'Honey, what you doin' with this heah white man?' "

71

"What do they call a guy who uses a pitchfork to shovel cement?"

"A mortar forker."

*     *     *

Hannah had been seeing Cazzy on and off for many years. Time passed and she had a child out of their union. Hannah met Cazzy by chance and told him she had named the baby Asphalt.

"Why'd you name him that?" he asked.

"Because," said Hannah, "it was my ass an' your fault!"

*     *     *

"Why won't you, honey?"

"I'm too tired."

"Ah, come on . . ."

"Leave me alone!"

"I won't be able to sleep."

"Well, I can't sleep now."

"Please."

"Why—in the middle of the night?"

" 'Cause I'm hot."

"You get hot at the damnedest times!"

"You don't love me!"

"Yes, I do . . ."

"If you loved me, you'd do it."

"Well dammit—all right."

"What's the matter?"

"I can't find it."

"That feels better!"

"It should be—it's all the way up."

"That's enough, thanks, dear."

"Next time, open the damn window yourself!"

\* \* \*

Sweet Charlie and Sally had been making it all night. In fact, for exactly forty-nine times. "Hey, baby," said Sweet Charlie, puffing on a cigarette, "let's do it one more time to make it an even fifty?"

"No way," stated Sally. "I'm sore."

"C'mon, honey, just once more!"

"No, I told you! We been doing it since ten o'clock last night. Every bone in my body aches. Forty-nine times is enough!"

Sweet Charlie got up, dressed, and as he walked out the door, looked at Sally and scowled: "So long, cold ass!"

\* \* \*

Two gals met in the supermarket. "You hear about Bessie Mae?"

"Naw, what?"

"I heard she was laid up in bed with that old lumbago!"

"No stuff? When did that son-of-a-bitch get back in town?"

Big Boomer came home and found his wife, Winona, naked and lying exhausted on a rumpled bed with a towel thrown over the foot.

"What's goin' on, honey?" he asked suspiciously.

"I just had the misery something terrible," she explained, "couldn't get outa bed all day."

"An' what's dat towel doin' there?"

"I wrang it out in water to put on my head, dat's all."

Boomer slowly pulled out a large razor and began stropping it.

"Whach you gonna do with dat razor?" asked Winona nervously.

"Effen dat towel dries out soft," said Boomer, "I'm gonna shave!"

\* \* \*

When John married Theresa, they moved into an old flat in Harlem. The first pieces of furniture the husband brought home were a big wash tub, a wash board and a full-length mirror.

"What's all that junk?" asked the wife.

"That's no junk—you take your choice. You take the tub and the wash board and go to work, or you take the mirror and sit down and watch yourself starve."

Lavinia the laundress shuffled into her mistress's study and hesitantly declared, "I won't be back after today. I've divorced that no-good skunk I married, and I'm going home to live with my folks."

"This is terrible news!" sighed her employer. "Who will wash for me now?"

"Don't be glum, ma'am," said Lavinia sympathetically, "that shiftless bastard of mine 'll find another wife before you know it!"

\* \* \*

## AFROLETIC SUPPORTER

*A Soul Brother's jock strap.*

\* \* \*

Sedgewich, a black swish, was speaking to some of his friends of the same race. He was attempting to drum up some business for a white friend who had just opened a gay bar in the Negro community.

"Listen!" swished Sedgewich, "that man's face may be white, but I tell you his heart is as black as any one of ours."

"Ilona, do you know anything of my wife's whereabouts?"

"Well, ah'm not sho', but I believe I put 'em in de wash."

Willie D. left Harlem to visit friends in Mobile. On his second night there he met Laura Mae, a beautiful lady whom he soon led out in the woods. As they prepared to make love, Willie removed his pants and hung them neatly on a tree.

"You must be from the North," said Laura Mae.

"Right on, baby," said Willie, "but how could you tell?"

"A Southern boy don't hang up his clothes 'cause when we're finished we're gonna be three miles from here."

* * *

Beverly Hills attorney Herb Schwartz tells about Sol Greenberg, the only Jewish man in a small Texas town. Greenberg was loved by everyone. He had given freely of his wealth and was particularly kind to the black population. And then Greenberg died.

Since he had no relatives, Greenberg bequeathed all his worldly goods to the townspeople. In order to show their respect and appreciation they decided to bury Greenberg in grand style.

They dressed him up in a cowboy outfit, complete with ten gallon hat and gold spurs. They had a solid gold Cadillac built, placed Greenberg behind the wheel and then dug a hole large enough to accommodate the car and its deceased occupant.

As they were lowering the Caddy into the ground, two Blacks stood nearby and one commented to the other, "Ah tell ya, man, them Jewish folks sure knows how to live!"

\*     \*     \*

Schmulowitz walked into the men's room at the Riviera Hotel in Las Vegas. As he stood at the urinals, seven-foot-tall Robertson came rushing in and unzipped his pants, revealing an enormous male endowment. Robertson proceeded to relieve himself.

"Wow!" he sighed with relief, "just made it!"

"You did?" asked Schmulowitz, glancing down at his companion. "Could you make me one in white?!"

\*     \*     \*

Rena went into the City Clerk's office to report the birth of her sixth child.

"But, miss, this is your sixth child by the same father," said the clerk. "Why don't you marry him?"

"Are you jivin'?" replied Rena. "I don't even like the sonuvabitch!"

Elmo drove Lena way out in the back woods, parked his car, and said, "Awright now, honey! Is you gonna be a Chesterfield and satisfy or are you gonna be a Camel and walk a mile?"

"Brother," said Lena, "it all depends on whether you is regular or king size!"

81

The census taker viewed Beatrice and the six tots of varying ages around her with a puzzled frown. Standing in the doorway of her fifth-floor Lenox Avenue apartment, he seemed particularly intrigued with a squirming infant in her arms.

"I don't quite understand you," said the census tallier. "Didn't you say your husband died six years ago?"

"Yes, sir," blustered Beatrice. "He died, but I didn't!"

*    *    *

Mavis applied for welfare. The clerk noticed on her application that she had a large assortment of children ranging in age from two to twenty. And that her husband had deserted her more than fourteen years before.

"How is it, Mrs. Green," asked the clerk, "that you have so many small children, yet you stated on your application for relief assistance that your husband deserted you more than fourteen years ago?"

"Oh, he did desert me, sir," replied Mavis. "But my husband is a sensitive man. So every once in a while he comes back in the middle of the night to say how sorry he is."

The schoolteacher was complaining rather bitterly to Cornelia about the behavior of little Nathaniel:

"He's always picking on boys smaller than he is and beating them up," she said.

"My goodness," said Cornelia, "that boy is jest like his pappy."

"And several times I've caught him in the cloakroom with one of the little girls," continued the teacher.

"Jest the sort of thing his pappy would do!" conceded Cornelia.

"Not only that, but he steals things from the other children."

"The very same as his pappy. Lord, ah sure am glad ah didn't marry that man!"

\*     \*     \*

Alma was being interviewed by the welfare officer concerning her application for relief.

"Are you married?"

"Yes, suh, ah been married twice."

"Any children?"

"Sho' has. Ah got six."

"All by the same father?"

"Nawsuh! Ah had two by mah first husband, two by mah second husband, and two without any help from nobody."

Ida Mae had been feeling out of sorts in the morning lately and went to see the doctor about it. After an examination the M.D. said, "You're going to get a visit from the stork. You'd better get your boyfriend to marry you if you can."

"But I don't have a boyfriend," said Ida Mae, "I live with my married sister and her husband."

"Hmm," pondered the physician. "What kind of sleeping arrangements do you have?"

"Well," said Ida Mae, "we all three sleeps in the same bed." Then thinking about it for a moment she added: "Say, doctor, do you 'spose ah could've got splashed?"

Two little colored boys met on the street.

"I'm five years old. How old are you?"

"I dunno."

"Do you ever think of women?"

"Naw!"

"Then you is four!"

\*     \*     \*

## HALF-BLACK, HALF-MEXICAN BELLY DANCER

*Bessie Mae Mucho*

\*     \*     \*

"Honey, how you feel 'bout messin' with men?"

"Well, if I likes 'em, I *lets* 'em—and if I loves 'em I *helps* 'em!"

\*     \*     \*

## COOL

*Is what you're keeping if the lady's husband walks in at the critical moment and you tell him, "Just a minute, daddy ...I'm almost finished."*

There is a place in the South where the law requires a man who gets a girl pregnant out of wedlock to pay a given sum of money every week for sixteen years to support the child.

A certain man had been faithfully making the payments for almost thirteen years. During the past two or three years, the mother had been sending the child to collect the money from her father.

One day, when the girl arrived, he smiled and said, "You go home and tell your mama that this is the final payment, and then watch the expression on her face."

The girl did as she was told, but was back in half an hour with the following message:

"I told Mama that this was the final payment and that you said I should watch the expression on her face. Well, she said, if this is the last payment, I should tell you that you're not my father, and I should watch the expression on YOUR face."

\* \* \*

JET SET

*What a Soul Brother carries in his jock strap.*

Mrs. Vandermeer learned that her husband made overtures to the black housekeeper and that he planned to go to her bed that night. Mrs. Vandermeer substituted for the housekeeper whom she sent across town on a late errand unexpectededly.

Later, she is boffed like never before. Finally satisfied physically, and now wanting her revenge, she snapped on the bedside lamp.

"I'll bet you're surprised!" she said triumphantly.

"Ah sure is, ma'am," said the black chauffeur in her arms.

While rambling along the railroad tracks, Isaac found twenty dollars. He walked on a little further and felt his corns pinch. "Feet," he said, "I'm gonna buy you a brand-new pair of shoes."

He continued his walk, but soon felt the hot sun on his forehead. "Old top," promised Isaac, "I'm gettin' you a cool, shady hat."

Just then Isaac's stomach grumbled. "Okay, belly," he said, "I will buy you a fine meal."

Isaac resumed his journey. Five minutes later, he stopped in shock. He looked downward at the front of his pants and hollered: "Hey, big stiff, who told *you* we came into money?"

\*      \*      \*

*Mistress:* Were you entertaining a man in the kitchen last night?

*Maid:* Well, ma'am, I was doin' my best.

\*      \*      \*

PFC Perkins refused to go and fight in Korea. He was told that if he would not bear arms the Provost Marshal would shoot him.

"Are you a conscientious objector?" asked the first Sergeant.

"I ain't objectin' to nothin'," said Perkins, "but I had the gonorrhea and the diarrhea both, and if this *Korea* is anything like it—go ahead and shoot!"

\* \* \*

"What makes you black men such good lovers?" asked the white employer of Kinney, the chauffeur.

"The trouble with you white folks is that you just go in there and rush, rush, rush, and before you know it, it's all over!" said Kinney. "Now the way us black folks do it, is get in there, take it easy, make long strokes, talk sweet a while, stop a while, take our time, then some more slow long strokes, nice and cool-like."

That night Whitey climbed into bed with his wife and began making love to her exactly as Kinney had suggested. After twenty minutes of sheer delight, she gasped, "My God! Where did you learn to screw like a black man?"

\* \* \*

## KEEP THE FAITH, BABY!

The congregation sat in awed silence as the preacher thundered: "God didn't make no hell down below! He'd already made Georgia, so why waste any more time and space?"

*     *     *

"How you like the new preacher?"
"Don't like him much. He preached so long I couldn't keep awake and he hollered so loud I couldn't go to sleep."

*     *     *

## SIGN ON CHURCH LAWN

*Don't Keep the Faith—Spread It Around*

Preacher Pitts had undertaken that morning to describe the terrors of hell to his congregation.

"Brothers and sisters," he intoned, "some of you have seen melted iron running out of a furnace, haven't you? It's white, sizzling, and hissing. Well, in the place I'm talking about, they use that stuff for ice cream."

\*  \*  \*

Dennison, a young, handsome Black boy had just died and arrived at the Pearly Gates wanting to enter.

"You got to be kidding," said St. Peter. "This place is strictly for heroes."

"Wait a minute," said Dennison. "You're talkin' to one of the greatest heroes of all time."

"What heroic thing did you do?"

"I married a white girl on the steps of the Biloxi, Mississippi City Hall at twelve noon."

"When did this happen?" asked St. Peter.

"Two minutes ago."

\*  \*  \*

| | |
|---|---|
| *Southern Preacher:* | Lissen here, y'all, if'n we is goin' to get money to build our church we is gotta work harder. Yo' gotta work like beavers to get sumthin' done. |
| *Sister Naomi:* | But pawson, beavers work with their tails. |
| *Preacher:* | Well, all reet! |

\* \* \*

In the old days down South, a minister had a Negro named Ezra in his household. Ezra was smart and ambitious, but he couldn't read or write.

One Sunday the minister saw Ezra in church, scribbling away industriously through the sermon. Afterward, the minister asked him:

"Ezra, what were you doing in church?"

"Takin' notes, suh. Ah's eaguh to l'arn."

"Let me see," said the minister, and he glanced over Ezra's notes, which looked more like Chinese than English.

"Why, Ezra," he chided, "this is all nonsense."

"Ah thought so," said Ezra, "all the time you was preachin' it."

Preacher Taylor had used the letters B.S., M.S., and Ph.D after his name for years without anyone from his congregation questioning it Finally, one morning after services, a nosey biddie asked him for some explanation.

"Well, sister," he answered, "you knows what B.S. stand foh, don't you?"

"Of course ah does," she replied indignantly.

"Well, then, that M.S. jest means 'more of same', and the Ph.D. means 'piled higher and deeper.' "

*     *     *

## NOTICE ON CHURCH BULLETIN BOARD

*Fellowship Dinner*—6:00 P.M.
*Healing Service*—7:00 P.M.

*     *     *

Parson Tatum was listening to a young man confess his sins. After ten minutes he stopped him.

"Wait a minute, young man," said the parson. "You ain't confessin'—you's braggin'."

*Deacon:* (To a new member after an outdoor baptism) Is the water cold, Nat?

*Nat:* No, not a bit cold.

*Deacon:* Better put him under again, Elder. He hasn't quit lying yet.

\* \* \*

Gratefully accepting the jar of home-made brandied pears from one of his elderly parishioners, the minister removed the lid, took a deep appreciative smell, and felt his legs wobble. "You don't know how much this affects me," he said, "and I thank you kindly."

"Oh," she said, "it's only a small present."

"It is not the present that counts," said the minister. "It is the spirit in which it is given."

\* \* \*

*Elder* (On departure of pastor from church): "Bretheren, we is gathered here to say goodbye to Brother Bradley, who has been our preacher now for fifteen years. He is leavin' on the next train for Shelbyville, and ah has been appointed by y'all to give him a little momentum."

96

Pastor Perry's congregation had forced him to quit. This Sunday was his farewell address. The church was packed.

"Owin' to the bad feelin' what exist 'tween mahself and suttin pussons in this congregation," he said with great dignity, "today's service terminates mah pastorate at this church.

"Ah will not say *'au revoir,'* 'cause that's a term used when friends take leave of each other. Ah will not say 'farewell,' 'cause that is too sad.

"But as ah promenades down the aisle towards the door, ah desire to call attention of the congregation to a sprig of mistletoe which am tied to the lower end of my coattail."

\*  \*  \*

The congregation had gathered at the riverbank for the baptismal services. It was winter, the river was frozen over, and a hole had been cut in the ice for the immersions. One of the women converts, on being dipped in the water, slipped from the preacher's grasp and was carried off downstream under the ice.

The preacher looked up calmly at the congregation.

"Brethren," he said, "this sister hath departed—hand me down another."

Comedian Jeremy Vernon, the Las Vegas sensation, sends this lighthearted lulu with love:

Burdened by years of poverty and prejudice, Jethro one day decided to speak directly to God.

"Oh, Lord," he said, "why did you give me this black skin?"

There was a flash of lightning and suddenly a voice from the heavens boomed: "To protect you from the burning rays of the tropical jungle sun."

"Lord," asked Jethro, "why did you give me this matty hair?"

"That," said the Creator, "is to enable you to escape your natural enemies and hunt your prey without getting your hair entangled in the thickets and the underbrush."

"Lord, why did you give me these wide nostrils?"

"To enable you to breathe oxygen from the hot, teaming humid air of the jungle."

"That all makes sense, Lord, but what am I doing here in Detroit?!"

\* \* \*

A traveling preacher in a strange town asked a newsboy the way to the post office. The boy showed him the route.

"Thank you!" said the preacher. "You seem to be a bright and courteous young man. How would you like to listen to my sermon this evening so that I may show you the way to Heaven?"

"You're going to show me the way to heaven?" declared the boy. "Why, you don't even know the way to the post office!"

* * *

The aged Negro preacher announced to his congregation: "Dar will be a baptism in dis chu'ch next Sabbath. Two adults an' six adulteresses is gwina be baptized."

* * *

"Miss Helen," said the parson impressively, as he led her into the brook for baptism, "I'se gwina lead you out inter dis heah stream, an' wash out ev'y spot er sin you'se got."

"Lawdy, Pahson," giggled the gal, "in that li'l ol' shallow creek?"

* * *

INVITATION TO A BAPTIST
CHURCH DINNER

*Come on in for a wing and a prayer*

Hattie and Aretha were standing on a street corner talking when two nuns passed. "Say," asked Hattie, "why do they call them ladies nuns?"

"Because," replied Aretha, "they ain't had none, they ain't got none, and they ain't never gonna get none."

"No wonder they wear mourning."

*   *   *

"Who will give the bride away?" asked the minister.

A man stood up. "I could," he said, "but I'm keepin' my mouth shut!"

*   *   *

The parson in a Southern town was asking his congregation to contribute as much money as they possibly could for the new church. Suddenly, the town prostitute stood up. "Reverend," she said, "I'd like to donate $2,500!"

"As much as we need funds," replied the minister, "ah refuse to accept tainted money."

"Take it, Reverend," shouted a male voice from the back of the church. "It's our money, anyway."

*Exhorter:* (At revival meeting) Come up en jine de Army ob de Lohd!

*Jefferson:* I'se done jined already.

*Exhorter:* Whar'd yoh jine?

*Jefferson:* In de Baptis' Chu'ch.

*Exhorter:* Why, chile, yoh ain't in the Army, yoh's in de Navy.

\* \* \*

Comedy writer Paul Pumpian passed on this plump piece of word play:

Reverend Walker stood before his congregation and in dynamic fashion pontificated on the wickedness of intercourse. After twenty minutes of ranting about the sin of sex, he raised himself to full height, leaned over the pulpit, and boomed:

"Brothers and sisters, if there are any among you who have committed adultery, may your tongue cleave to the woof of your mowf."

\* \* \*

Why aren't there any black nuns?

Because they find it difficult to say Superior after Mother.

Parson Denson after his Sunday service went out the back door of the church and stumbled upon two boys masturbating.

"Now you boys keep that up and you gonna go blind!"

"Okay," whispered one boy to the other, "let's just do it till we need glasses!"

\*     \*     \*

"Is thah any among you bredren," asked the mountain preacher, "that has had some experience with ghosts?"

"I has," answered Archie.

"What kind of experience, brother?"

"Intercourse," replied Archie.

"You mean to say y'all had intercourse with a ghost?"

"Ah beg yo' pahdon," he replied. "Ah thought you said GOATS."

\*     \*     \*

*Dennis:* The preacher used very poor judgment this mornin'.
*Oscar:* How was that?
*Dennis:* He preached on "A Fool and His Money Are Soon Parted," right *before* the collection.

Raymond, the sinner, lay dying and he asked that the minister come to his bedside.

"Reverend," whispered Raymond, "I have not been a churchgoer and the world may not forgive my sins. But tell me that God will."

"Perhaps He will," said the minister comfortingly. "After all, He didn't get to know you the way we did."

*     *     *

A visiting minister had been invited to conduct the service and preach the sermon at the small Southern Baptist church in Mississippi. After the sermon, the hat was passed to help defray the traveling expenses of the visiting preacher.

It came back empty, save for three pennies.

The minister took the hat, fell to his knees, raised his eyes to Heaven, and intoned:

"Dear God, I am truly thankful this day that I have been granted by Thee the good fortune of getting my hat back from this congregation. Amen. And good day, brothers!"

"Brethren," said the elder of a Southern church. "Brethren, ah got a five-dollar sermon, an' a two-dollar sermon, an' a one-dollar sermon, an' I wants this here meretricious audience to take up a collection as to which one of them they can afford to hear."

\* \* \*

"Brothers," said the colored preacher, "the subject of my sermon today is 'Liars.' How many in this congregation have read the sixty-ninth chapter of Matthew?" Nearly every hand went up.

"You are the very people I want to preach to," the reverend said. "There is no such chapter."

\* \* \*

Pastor Barnes was an old-fashioned preacher who had been taking his membership and congregation to task for what he considered acts of dishonesty.

After abusing them for a while, he concluded:

"Of course, our people is the best people in the world. But the trouble with you is, that the white man done been dealing with you so long, some of you is gettin' real tricky."

*Parson* (in fervent prayer): "Oh, Lord, dis here little congregation of mine am prone to gossip! Oh, Lord, dis here little congregation of mine am prone to bear false witness!

"Oh, Lord, dis here little congregation of mine am prone to steal!

"Oh, Lord, dis here little congregation of mine am prone to do things what am wrong in de house of de Lord!

"And, good Lord! I am askin' you to deliver them from de prone!"

\*     \*     \*

*Minister:* Young man, please do not give me a ticket. Ah'm just a poor preacher.

*Policeman:* Yes, ah know. Ah've heard you.

\*     \*     \*

A Holy Roller prayer meeting was in full swing down South. Sister Sara, the most comely gal in the entire congregation, leaped to her feet and shouted: "Praise be! Las' night ah was in de arms of Satan and tonight ah is in de arms of Saint Peter!"

"Sister," said a brother who had been sitting beside her, "how is you fixed up fo' tomorrow night?"

A missionary came into a section of Africa where he had never been before and met the chief of a cannibal tribe. "Do your people know anything about religion?" he asked.

"Well," said the cannibal, "we got a little taste of it when the last missionary was here!"

A preacher was asked who came first, the black man or the white man. "Well, brothers and sisters," said the minister, "it all happened like this:

"The first man the Lord made was named Adam. The first woman was called Eve. They had two children, Cain and Abel. The Ma and Pa and those two chil'ren were black. Now, Cain was a bad one, always shootin' and cuttin' folks, and gamblin'. He was jealous of his brother Abel, and he killed him one day in a fight over the best watermelon patch.

"Then the Lord came up behind Cain and says to him: 'Cain, where's your brother?'

"That Cain was a sassy one, so he didn't even turn around to see who it is, but just answers up biggity, 'Am I my brother's keeper? I ain't got him in my pocket. I s'pose he's off somewhere shootin' craps.'

"That got the Lord angry. 'Cain, where's your brother!' thundered the Lord.

"Cain whirled around and when he saw it was the Lord he got so scared his hair stood right up straight and his face turned right pale.

"And sisters and brothers, that is where the first white man came from!"

*   *   *

# ARE YOU ALL WHITE?

Too bad, because some of this black humor
may be just too funny to bear. But let your
true sense of soul guide you . . . and you'll
get a lot of laughs out of these pages. It's all
in black and white, baby, how discriminating
can you get?

# THE OFFICIAL WHITE FOLKS JOKE BOOK

### by Larry Wilde

PINNACLE BOOKS  •  NEW YORK CITY

# THE
# OFFICIAL
# WHITE FOLKS
# JOKE BOOK

# INTRODUCTION

The last time Bob Hope did a sketch about plumbers on his television show he received hundreds of letters protesting his attack on the plumbing profession.

In an effort to avoid such discontent among his viewers, the great comedian immediately instructed the writing staff to devise gags about a group that would take his good-natured kidding a little more broad-mindedly.

The next show, Hope did a sketch chiding doctors. Within seventy-two hours Bob and the TV network were inundated by angry letters and telegrams from physicians and surgeons. They fiercely objected to the "modern-day Will Rogers" taking pot shots at the honorable profession of medicine.

1

It is common practice for comedians to pick on people (the Dean Martin "Roasts" are some of the most popular shows on the tube). Television aside, the art of story telling is on the upswing once again, for even cocktail party goers are spinning yarns about Poles, Italians, Jews, Blacks, Mexicans, Chinese, Indians, and Irishmen.

However, ethnic and minority groups are not the only people being used as the butt of the barbed jest. Joke tellers also poke fun at folks because they are *rebels*, or *hillbillies* or *hicks* or *city slickers* and even *politicians*. It seems no one escapes the sharp comedic needle required to prick the bubble of pomposity and thereby provoke a guffaw.

Even during the height of entertainment on the stage in this country, the nation's vaudeville houses demanded strict adherence to their code of restrictions. Witness this sign backstage at a Midwestern theater:

NO BLUE MATERIAL. NO JOKES LOUSING UP THE TOWN OR THE TROLLEY OR THE RAILROAD. AND NO FOUL PUNCH LINES IN SONGS OR
*You Will Be Cancelled*

As comedy performers traveled the four corners of America it became evident that each region had its own particular sense of humor. Comics soon discovered they could go over much bigger with audiences in the South doing rural and farm jokes.

West of the Mississippi, gags about cowpokes, Indians, mules, and horses could be counted on as great laugh grabbers. Up North, through Illinois, Michigan, and Minnesota, the jesters relied on jokes about cold weather, Swedes, and city life. In the East, they again added material to fit crowds. Here's one that covered two sections of the country at once:

*He was from New England, with his nasal twang. She was from Georgia, with her Southern drawl. And, Oh, how he loved to get his twang caught in her drawl.*

Regional humor is fun. It is one of the cultural contributions that has helped mold America. Imagine being able to tell what part of the country someone comes from simply by that person's speech pattern. Witness this dialogue:

*A Brooklyn boy asked his buddy, "Do you know how cattle breed?"*

*"Yeah," replied his pal, "dey breed troo dare noses."*

This viable vignette makes its own point:

*Paul, Jack, and Bill had become buddies in the army. Now many years later they were having a reunion at a New York hotel. One night the boys met a beautiful girl and they were saying goodnight.*

*"Just a moment," said the gorgeous girl to Paul. "Where are you from?"*

*"I'm from the East!" he replied.*

*"Very well, you may kiss my right hand." She turned to Jack. "And where are you from?"*

*"I'm from the West!" he declared.*

*"All right," said the girl, "you may kiss my left hand." Now it was Bill's turn.*

*"And you?" she purred.*

*"Well, ma'am, I just ain't gonna answer y'all!"*

At the risk of sharing Bob Hope's fate at the hands of letter-writing fanatics, I invite you to enjoy the following funnies. Between these covers you will find gags and quips and jokes and stories representing every part of our great nation. Even Texas.

If you can't take a trip across the U.S.A. here's a chance to visit America from your armchair and have a good laugh while doing it.

LARRY WILDE
September 1975

## THE NORTH

A hard-hat redneck who worked in a nearby Pittsburgh steel mill was finishing his tenth beer at a corner saloon. The alcohol so loosened his tongue that he slammed his fist down on the bar and shouted:

"I'm a good American. There's only two things in this country I can't stand —race prejudice and Negroes!"

\* \* \*

A black man and a white man were drinking beer in a bar. They were watching Notre Dame playing football on television.

"Hey, Willie," said the white, "look at that!" They got a black guy playing for Notre Dame!"

"Sure, man! Ain't you never heard of an Irish jig?!"

How do you stop five blacks from raping a white woman in Detroit?

Throw them a basketball!

\*　　\*　　\*

The automobile industry has literally
turned the motor city into eight-hour
shifts. Two workmen at an assembly
plant, Mac a black, and Carl a white,
were changing shifts. "You sure have a
pretty wife," said Mac to his replace-
ment.

"Did you ever see her first thing in
the morning?" sneered Carl.

"No," answered Mac, "she always
makes me pull out before you come in
off the night detail."

\*　　\*　　\*

General Motors is coming out with a
new compact Cadillac designed especially for out-of-work Negroes.

\*　　\*　　\*

A man went into a bar and ordered
a beer. After he'd been served, he
reached into his breast pocket and lifted
out a perfectly formed little figure four
inches tall. Then he produced a thimble.

"A beer for my friend Paul, here, too," he requested, "and go easy on the head."

"Is he for real?" asked the bartender.

"He is," said the man.

"Can he talk?" persisted the barkeep.

"He can," replied the man. "Paul," he went on, "tell this guy about the time we were on that expedition and you called the witch doctor a black son-of-a-bitch."

\* \* \*

Payne and Butler were washing their hands in a Pittsburgh men's room when three burly blacks came in and headed for the urinals.

"Wow!" whispered Payne, "those mother's are laa-arge!"

"Yeah," said Butler, "and look how they're built. They must have the longest dicks in the state of Pennsylvania. I gotta get closer and see their size!"

He came back in a minute. "Whowee! They are built big," said Payne," not only that, the cat in the middle has one that's white!"

"Oh, man, whoever heard of a black man with a white wang! I'm gonna go look myself."

He returned immediately. "Brother, those cats ain't black!" exclaimed Butler. "They're Polish coal miners! And the guy in the middle is on his honeymoon!"

What would you call a Negro maternity dress manufacturer?

A mother frocker.

\* \* \*

Crawford passed a tavern that had a sign in the window: *We Serve* WHITES *Only*.

He entered the saloon anyway, sat at the bar and ordered a whiskey. The bartender rushed to the rear of the tavern and reminded the boss of the *We Serve* WHITES *Only* sign.

"Never mind," said the owner. "Serve him his drink but charge him twenty bucks for it!"

Ten minutes later, Crawford ordered another whiskey. Again the bartender approached his employer, who said, "Okay, give it to him, but charge him fifty dollars!"

Soon Crawford ordered another drink. This time the boss said to the barkeep, "Charge him a hundred dollars a shot!"

As the bartender started to leave the owner added: "And change that sign in the window to: *We Serve* BLACKS *Only*"

\* \* \*

What would you call a Negro cravat maker?

A tie-coon.

Whitehead came home one cold winter night to find his golden-blonde wife on the living-room divan deep in the loving arms of a big dark Negro. Petrified, in his astonishment Whitehead forgot to close the front door. The icy winds rushed in.

Thinking his wife was being raped, he shouted in a frenzy, "Darling, what shall I do to this Negro?"

"Shut the door quick," cried the wife, "so he won't catch cold."

\*   \*   \*

A Minneapolis housewife returned from her morning shopping. "How's the weather outside?" asked her husband.

"Cold enough," she answered, "to test your frosticles."

\*   \*   \*

They were screwing in old Minnesota
When she said, "you've exceeded your
    quota,
  We have grooved for an hour,
  You have proved you have power
Ain't you *ever* gonna turn off your
    mota?"

11

She had an Indiana figure—a large South Bend.

*   *   *

Comedian-producer-writer Sid Miller proposed this bit of buffoonery:

In a small Indiana town, Evans was waiting at an intersection for the yearly circus parade to pass by. He saw a sign on one of the wagons that read:

## BARNEY'S CIRCUS WITH FIFTY ELEPHANTS

He counted the pachyderms as they crossed the intersection. When he got to fifty, Evans put his car in gear and started to cross the street. Unfortunately, he had miscounted and his car hit and killed the last elephant.

A week later Evans got a notice from the circus that he'd have to pay $300,-000. He telephoned the circus manager.

"Hey," he roared, "I hit only one lousy elephant. Why do you want $300,-000?"

"It's true you hit only one elephant," replied the manager, "but you pulled the tails out of forty-nine others!"

# HUNGARIAN

*Well-equipped guy from Gary, Indiana.*

\*　　\*　　\*

Gil Miller, the successful Skokie, Illinois, theatrical booker, once did a novelty act. Here's a scene Gil overheard while working an Ohio nightspot:

Roger, the sharpie salesman, was in Cleveland for just the one night. He figured he'd have to work fast. He was dancing with a pretty nurse he had just met at the bar, and started in for the kill.

Roger held her very close. "You're lovely," he whispered. "You set me on fire."

Roger gave her another squeeze and said: "You're a marvelous dancer!"

He nuzzled her and murmured: "In fact, you're the most fantastic dancer I've ever met."

A few minutes went by and he started in again. "Look, honey, this is the only night I'm going to be spending in this city."

"That's a shame. You'll only be in Cleveland tonight!" she said. "Tell you what, I'll dance as fast as I can!"

Chicago, the great convention city, provides every kind of entertainment for its visitors, even those who must stay longer than a few days.

After six weeks away on business the married exec entered a West Side brothel. He walked up to the madam, handed her a hundred dollar bill, and said, "I want the worst screw in the house."

"But, sir," answered the madam, "one hundred dollars will buy you our best."

"No," demanded the businessman, "I want the worst available."

"I can't let you do this," the woman pleaded. "You're entitled to the top of the line."

"Listen, lady," said the man, "I'm not horny, just homesick."

15

The wind can become mighty fierce in Chicago's Loop. Imagine the surprise of a man seeing a woman actually holding her dress over her head.

"Shame on you," said the man with a smile.

"Listen, young man," said the woman, "what you're looking at is sixty-five years old, but this hat's brand-new!"

\*     \*     \*

Fred Allen was one of the most creative comedians in show business. Here's a line he wrote that has become a classic:

"I once spent a summer vacation at a little seacoast town in Maine. This little town was so dull that one day the tide went out and never came back."

\*     \*     \*

TV host Jack Narz tells about Jeb and Nemiah, two stern-faced Bangor men who went fishing one day in an old boat. For three hours neither of them moved a muscle. Then Jeb, sitting aft, got restless.

"Doggone it, Jeb, that's the third time you shuffled your feet in an hour," said Nemiah. "You come out here to fish or practice dancing?"

There is a young lady in Maine,
Whose face is exceedingly plain.
    But down in her cellar,
    She's a real live heller,
So the boys come again and again.

\*       \*       \*

A dignified, matter-of-fact Vermonter entered a department store. Suddenly, music, photographers, and TV cameras appeared like magic. A smiling master of ceremonies rushed to his side and informed him he was the lucky three millionth customer.

"And now, will you tell us and the TV audience what you came here for today?"

"Gladly," answered the customer. "I'm on my way to the Complaint Department."

\*       \*       \*

The hard-bitten Rutland farmer greeted the news of his wife's pregnancy without the flick of a facial muscle.

"Ain't a bit surprised," he said to the doctor. "I've given her every opportunity."

Wept a music-mad matron from Maine,
"When I water, it patters like rain.
How I wish I could *pio*
The *'O Sole Mio,'*
Or the rhythmical rush of a train!"

\* \* \*

Real estate millionaire Robert Glazer gets guffaws with this goodie:

Arguments still rage between Texas and Alaska for "bigness honors" in the U.S.A. One time there was a seven-foot Texan on holiday in Alaska. He walked into the only department store in Nome and asked for a winter coat for himself.

"Yes, sir!" said the clerk. "Second floor, Boy's Wear."

\* \* \*

A tourist in Nome, Alaska, seeing his first Eskimos, noticed a native mother with a blonde, blue-eyed baby slung to her back and asked, "Is your child a full-blooded Eskimo?"

"Half," the native replied.

"Half Irish? Half Scotch? Half what?" asked the tourist.

"Half Coast Guard," replied the mother.

An icy wind blew fiercely in the Arctic Circle. Across the wastes appeared a dogsled. Its occupants were a pretty little Eskimo girl and a big strong Eskimo youth.

"Mush," said the girl.

"Mush!" said the boy.

And while they were mushing, someone stole the dogsled.

*       *       *

Did you know that Admiral Peary's dog went crazy looking for the North Pole?

*       *       *

Advertising executive Marci Muhleman tells about the couple registering at a small hotel in Vermont who were asked to show their wedding license. The man flashed a fishing license to the nearsighted clerk and laid it on the desk.

After the couple went upstairs the clerk examined the license more carefully and rushed up after them.

He banged on the door shouting: "If you ain't done it, don't do it! This ain't the license fer it!"

Some Alaskan miners in a Fairbanks bar were kidding Barrows, a visiting oilman from Abilene, about his state's being the second biggest in the Union.

"Texas may not be the biggest state," said Barrows, "but it's still the toughest!"

"Toughest!" cried one of the miners. "Why, in Alaska we don't consider a man a man unless he can down a fifth of whiskey in one pull at the bottle, wrestle a grizzly bear with his bare hands, and rape an Eskimo woman—all in one night!"

"Say," said the Lone Star oilman, "I'd be willin' to bet I could do that!"

So a wager was made. Barrows took a full fifth of whiskey and downed it in one long swallow.

"All right," he said, "where do I find me a grizzly bear?"

"The mountains just outside town are full of bears," explained one of the miners. "You'll have no trouble finding one."

Barrows stalked out into the night. Two hours later, he came staggering back into the bar. His clothes were in shreds, his body a mass of bloody cuts and bruises.

"All right, now," said the Texan. "Where's the Eskimo woman you want me to wrestle?"

Irv Auerbach, the hydroponic tomato tycoon, tells this tale of two prospectors trying their luck in the Klondike:

Gannon and Barker arrived in Alaska to search for gold. Their first stop was the Last Frontier General Store. Here they purchased all the necessary supplies and equipment needed for their trip.

Then, at the storekeeper's suggestion, they also bought love-boards. These were small pine boards cut in the outline of a woman's shape, with a fur-lined knothole in the middle.

Several months later, Gannon landed in New York alone.

"What happened to your partner?"

"I had to kill him," said Gannon. "I caught the son-of-a-bitch using my love-board."

\* \* \*

# THE EAST

At a New York hospital maternity ward, the nurse came out with a little blonde baby and held it up. Swenson, one of the three men awaiting news of their wives' births, jumped up and shouted: "Dot's mine!"

A few minutes later the woman in white returned holding a little dark-haired babe. "Thatsa mine!" said Giordano.

In a while the nurse returned with a black baby. Murphy stood up and said, "Begorrah! That one belongs to me!"

"Are you sure?" asked the incredulous nurse.

"Oh, yes," said Murphy. "My wife burns everything!"

Anything can happen in Manhattan. Last week, in the Lexington Avenue subway, a weirdo flung open his overcoat to expose himself to a black lady.

"Please, not tonight!" she exclaimed. "I've got a headache!"

*　　*　　*

In Brooklyn, what is the difference between a pickpocket and a peeping Tom?

A pickpocket snatches watches.

*　　*　　*

If the garbage workers in your community ever go out on strike, you might like to know how an enterprising New Yorker got rid of his refuse during the nine days of the "Great New York Garbage Strike."

Each day he wrapped his garbage in gift paper. Then he put it in a shopping bag. When he parked his car, he left the bag on the front seat with the window open. When he got back to the car, the garbage had always been collected.

*　　*　　*

NEW YORK
*Where the cab meters go faster than the cabs.*

A reporter from a Westchester newspaper on an assignment in Greenwich Village struck up a conversation with a young lady in a bar. After a few drinks he suggested they buy a bottle and go to his room. She agreed.

Thirty minutes later, the girl began taking off her clothes. "Say, how old are you?" asked the reporter.

"Thirteen!" she retorted.

"Thirteen! Good Lord! You get those clothes back on and get out of here!"

At the door the teenager paused and said, "Superstitious, eh?"

\*     \*     \*

On a crowded subway, a well-built mulatto secretary felt behind her the presence of a sexually excited soul brother. She tried to move away, but her fidgeting only made things worse. Finally she turned around and snapped, "Mister! You are vulgar!"

"I didn't do nothin' wrong, honey!" said the black man. "But I can understand why you're a little peeved. I got paid tonight, the boss had nothing but small change, and it makes a lump in my pants pocket. Believe me, baby, that's all there is to it."

"I suppose," said the woman, "you also want me to believe that all the time we are standing here, your *boss* is giving you raises!"

There was a young lady named Gloria
Than whom there was none horia
   She was had by six men
   Again and again
And the band at the Waldorf-Astoria.

\*　　\*　　\*

Seymour Wildman, world traveler and bon vivant, tells about the tourist visiting New York.

Walking on a side street late one evening, the visitor was held up by a bandit. "Give me your money," he threatened, "or I'll blow out your brains."

"Blow away," said the tourist, "in New York you can live without brains, but not without money."

\*　　\*　　\*

The New York City Chief of Police spoke before a large women's club. "Do you know that in your city, a woman is raped every four and a half hours?"

The stunned silence was broken by one of the younger members who exclaimed: "She must be the happiest woman in the world."

# OVERHEARD AT GRAND CENTRAL STATION

"You're the best little wife a guy ever had—even if your husband doesn't think so."

* * *

Only in New York can you find the super-educated snob and the sordid salesman sitting side-by-side on bar-stools.

Simmons had been drinking all night at Barney's Grill and now he was pretty well soused. Suddenly he created a rude odoriferous zephyr.

A man sitting on the next stool jumped up, grabbed him, and said, "How dare you flatulate before my wife?"

"Sorry, buddy," sputtered Simmons. "I didn't realize it was her turn."

* * *

A girl who came East from the farm
Exclaimed, "City life has its charm,
  Take the pleasures of orgasm:
  Ev'ry girl in New York has 'em,
But in Kansas they're viewed with
    alarm."

# BRONX VIRGIN

*Any girl who doesn't have an illegitimate child.*

\*    \*    \*

A section of Manhattan called the Bowery, home to winos and derelicts, has become the most famous Skid Row in the world. Here's one of the reasons why:

At four o'clock in the morning a drunk staggered into a Bowery flophouse shouting, "I'm Jesus Christ! I'm Jesus Christ!"

The sleeping men were all awakened. "I'm Jesus Christ! I'm Jesus Christ!" blurted the wino.

"Ah, shut up!" howled the hotel inhabitants. "Be quiet!"

"I'm Jesus Christ!" slobbered the inebriate. "I'm Jesus Christ!"

"Will you let us get some sleep!"

"If you don't believe me, come on downstairs and I'll prove it to you!"

A few of the men got up and followed him outside where he walked up to a darkened saloon and began bellowing and banging on the door.

The proprietor who lived upstairs heard the noise, came down, and opened

the front door. He looked at the drunk and shouted, "Jesus Christ, are you here again?"

"You see, I told you!" said the drunk turning to his followers.

*     *     *

Foster sat in the posh offices of Park Avenue's most famous physician. "I've got this terrible problem," he explained. "Everything I eat turns to gas. I just had steak and potatoes and it turned to gas."

"That could be serious," countered the doctor.

"But fortunately," said Foster, "my gas is noiseless and odorless. Can you cure it?"

"I'm sure that I'll be able to help. But first I'm going to fit you with a hearing aid and then I'm going to fix your nose."

*     *     *

At dances, a girl from Connecticut
Showed an absolute absence of eticut,
    Letting all comers press
    Thru the skirt of her dress,
And then mopping the mess with her
        peticut.

## SIGN ON A JERSEY
## MILK TRUCK

*All I Am I Owe to Udders*

\* \* \*

## SARATOGA, N.Y.

*Where the baths clean you in the morning and the track cleans you in the afternoon.*

\* \* \*

A sextet of gay flutists and their manager rented a seaside cottage on Fire Island. The neighbors refer to the place as *The House of Seven Gobbles.*

\* \* \*

## SIGN APPROACHING
## FIRE ISLAND

*Stamp Out Mental Health*

\* \* \*

Here's to dear old Boston
The land of the bean and the cod,
Where the Lowells speak only to Cabots
And the Cabots speak only to God.

Guy Livingston, Bean Town's veteran *Variety* staffer, passed on this bit of badinage:

A garment center salesman on a business trip to Boston had a few hours to kill before catching a plane home. Remembering an old friend's advice to try some broiled scrod, a favorite fish in Boston, he hopped into a cab.

"Say," he said to the driver, "do you know where I could get scrod around here?"

"Mister," replied the young cabby, a Harvard undergraduate, "I've heard that question a thousand times, but this is the first time in the pluperfect subjunctive."

\*　　\*　　\*

In the municipal offices there was a rule. Only Harvard graduates could be promoted above a certain level. The last three college men to assume responsible jobs with the administration bungled their efforts badly. Their departments were a mess.

This sign finally appeared just over the toilet paper dispenser in the city hall men's room: HARVARD UNIVERSITY DIPLOMAS—TAKE ONE.

In Boston, they live on beans.
In Seattle, they live on the Sound.

\*     \*     \*

Accountant Ken Gerstenfeld tells about the New York banking house that wrote a Boston investment firm requesting a letter of recommendation about a young Bostonian they were considering for a job.

The investment concern could not say enough about the young man. "His father," they wrote, "was a Cabot, his mother, a Lowell; further back his background was a happy blend of Saltonstalls, Appletons, Peabodys, and others of Boston's First Families."

"The information supplied is inappropriate," replied the New York company. "We are not contemplating using the young man for breeding purposes."

\*     \*     \*

The lady from Boston said, "In Boston we place our emphasis entirely on breeding."

And the lady from Philadelphia said, "In Philadelphia, we think it's a lot of fun, but we do other things, too."

## WASHINGTON, D.C.

*They have statues of all the great politicians there. They even have one of Napoleon. But you can tell he wasn't a politician. He's got his hand in his own pocket.*

\* \* \*

A topless Go-Go dancer in Newark refers to herself as "The Jersey Bounce."

\* \* \*

*Jack:* Were you ever inside the Mammoth Cave?

*Mack:* Yes, but don't let my wife hear you call it that.

\* \* \*

A Brooklyn boy ready to boist
Shacked up wit' a French goil, his foist,
   When she said, "Ah! Mon cher!"
   He replied, "Stop right dere!
Would you radder we screwed or convoist?"

\* \* \*

## STOIC

*De boid dat brings da babies.*

Philadelphians have always been noted for their striving toward perfection, as the following story illustrates:

Fenton, visiting the City of Brotherly Love, decided to dine in Philadelphia's most exclusive restaurant.

"Your order?" asked the waiter.

"I'll have the hamburger plate," replied Fenton after examining the menu.

In a few minutes the waiter returned. He uncovered a casserole dish revealing two hamburgers. From a pocket the waiter produced a pair of silver tongs and with them he transferred the meat patties to the diner's plate.

"We never touch anything with our hands," said the waiter, smiling.

"Very nice," said Fenton.

"Cleanliness is our motto," retorted the waiter. "And we never touch anything with our hands."

"That's wonderful!"

"We even have a special rule about visiting the lavatory. See this little piece of string attached to my apron?"

"I noticed all the waiters had them. What's it for?"

"Well," said the waiter, placing a large potato on Fenton's plate with his silver tongs, "if I have to go to the bathroom, I just unzip my pants and take it out with that piece of string. That way everything stays sanitary."

34

"But how do you put it back?" asked Fenton.

"I don't know about the other men," said the waiter, "but I use these tongs. We never touch anything with our hands."

*   *   *

## GREENWICH VILLAGE

*Where every man has a chance to be Queen for a Day.*

*   *   *

Stanley and Christopher met at a Greenwich Village Eighth Street gay bar. "Haven't seenya around, lately," lisped Stanley. "Been missingya."

"I've been in the hospital for an operation," retorted Christopher. "Got circumcised. Take a look."

"It's just adorable," said Stanley. "Makes you look ten years younger!"

*   *   *

## GAY BLADE

*The Fire Island fencing champion.*

Charles and Randolph were sitting in the last row of Waverly place theater watching a horror movie.

"Ain't it gruesome?" whispered Charles.

"It sure has!" responded Randolph.

\*   \*   \*

Edwards arrived in New York seeking his fame and fortune. As he strolled down the sidewalk, he noticed a great long ladder propped against the side of the building, stretching upward as far as the eye could see. Edwards started to pass on by, but a voice high in the clouds called down, "CLIMB UP THE LADDER TO SUCCESS!"

Somewhat nervously, Edwards began to ascend, rung by rung, all the way to the top of a fifty-story edifice. When he got there, a slender, blond, blue-eyed boy seated on the ledge of the building smiled sweetly at him.

"Hi, there!" he said. "I'm CESS!"

\*   \*   \*

Cedric, an obvious limp wrist type, tippy-toed up to a streetwalker in Times Square.

"Hi, prostitute," he sneered.

"Hi, substitute!" she retorted.

"I rang your doorbell this morning but you wouldn't come to the door," said Sumner to his friend.

"I heard you," replied Rory, "and I called to you that I was busy with a friend."

"If you were really busy, how could you call out to me?"

\* \* \*

Doris and Myrna, two Manhattan prosties, decided to bolster their sagging business in the Yellow Pages.

Doris went under FUN AND GAMES.

Myrna took a listing in SPORTING EQUIPMENT.

\* \* \*

A former secretary turned hooker bumped into an old school chum. "How can you go into such a profession?" asked her friend.

"Don't be silly," answered the call girl. "We provide a vital service. We're a wife to those who have none, and a refuge to those who do."

One night recently a Park Avenue house of pleasure was raided and the girls were taken outside and lined up for questioning by the police. A little old lady happened to be passing by and asked, "What's going on?"

As a joke, one of the girls said, "We're standing in line for free lollipops!"

A few minutes later a policeman approached the elderly woman. "Aren't you a bit old for this?" he asked.

"Officer," she gummed, "as long as they keep making them, I'll keep sucking them."

# NEW YORK SUBWAY SIGN

*Help keep prostitutes off the streets.*
*Take them to your apartment.*

\* \* \*

Did you hear about the airline stewardess who turned to prostitution?
She greeted all her customers with "Welcome aboard!"

\* \* \*

Sally and Jane, two ladies of the evening, were strolling down Fifth Avenue. "I just love working this street," said Sally. "It's always so exciting."
"You don't have to tell me about it," replied Jane. "I'm sold on it myself."

\* \* \*

New Jersey restaurateur Martin Wogansky used to delight customers at his Wildwood Deli with this dilly:
Murray stopped his car on a deserted country road, slid over beside his date, and began making obvious advances. "Just a minute," declared the girl,

pushing him away, "I'm really a prostitute and I have to charge you fifty dollars."

Murray paid her and they made love.

Later, he sat motionless behind the wheel. "Aren't we leaving?" asked the hooker.

"Not quite yet," replied Murray. "I'm really a cab driver and the fare back is fifty dollars."

*   *   *

# THE SOUTH

A Negro's body was found on the outskirts of a small Mississippi town. The victim had been bound hand and foot, stabbed seventeen times, and had six bullet wounds in his body.

"What's your verdict, sheriff?" asked a reporter.

"Worst case of suicide I ever saw!" replied the lawman.

*    *    *

A prominent North Carolina planter was sitting with his daughter enjoying his mint julep on the front porch of his white-columned mansion.

"Daddy," she said.

"Yes, my Belle of the South?"

"I'm plannin' to get married, Daddy."

"Well, this is a surprise, Sugar Cane. Who's the lucky man?"

"His name is Harry Belafonte."

"Harry Belafonte? Now honey I told you 'bout foolin' around with them Eye-talians!"

*   *   *

There was a white bigot in Birmingham who was a bedwetter. He used to go to his Klan meetings in rubber sheets.

*   *   *

Before his daring escape from prison, a black militant had been photographed from four different angles. The FBI sent copies of the pictures to police chiefs all across the country, with orders to notify Washington the moment an arrest was made.

The next day the bureau received a teletyped reply from the ambitious sheriff of a small Southern town:

PICTURES RECEIVED.
ALL FOUR SHOT DEAD
WHILE RESISTING ARREST.

A Macon matron living near an army camp decided to do her duty as a good citizen and invite some G.I.s over for lunch.

"I'd like you to send over a dozen nice soldier boys," she said over the phone. "But I don't want any Jews!"

An hour later there was a knock at her door and in walked a dozen Blacks. "Th-there m-must be some m-mistake!" sputtered the woman.

"There's no mistake, ma'am," replied the corporal in charge. "General Ginsberg never makes a mistake!"

# GEORGIA GENTLEMAN

*A fellow who will make love to the maid in his wife's bed, when his wife is away on a trip, and then makes the maid ride in the backseat when he drives her home.*

\*     \*     \*

A society girl from the better part of Boston became a Vista Volunteer and was sent to work in the Mississippi Bayous. While there, she fell in love with a young black medic assigned to the Free Public Health Clinic. Not quite knowing how to break this news to her folks, the girl wrote home:

"Dear Mom and Dad:

*I have met a wonderful man, a doctor. He comes from a one-horse town, and it's a horse of a different color ..."*

\*     \*     \*

Black baseball pitchers Ferguson Jenkins and Jim Bibby of the Texas Rangers drove to training camp together and stopped at a roadside restaurant in a backwoods area in Georgia.

"I don't think we better go in there," said Bibby after looking the place over.

"Why not?" asked Jenkins.

"Because," said Bibby with a straight face, "they might not know you're Canadian."

Did you hear about the elderly Alabama schoolmarm who thought that Shirley Temple Black was a Negro Synagogue?

*     *     *

Way back in the days of slavery, a Georgia plantation owner lived openly with a beautiful black slave girl. His neighbors were jealous for obvious reasons but they were also angry out of "race pride." They complained and accused him of believing in racial equality.

"But that's a damned lie," protested the plantation owner. "It's true I stay with her a lot, but I'll be damned if I'll let her eat at the table with me."

*     *     *

Two Blacks found themselves in a small hotel in Mississippi with a long evening ahead and nothing to do.

"Why don't we call the desk," suggested one, "and have them send up a couple of white girls?"

"Are you crazy?" exclaimed his friend. "Ask for white girls in Mississippi?"

"Why not?" said the first. "I'm just figuring on making love to them. I don't plan to go to school with them."

An African ambassador asked for a room in a Southern hotel.

"We don't have rooms for your kind," replied the clerk.

"I didn't want the room for myself," explained the diplomat. "It's for my wife, and she is your kind."

A Southern plantation owner bought a monkey from a pet shop as a gift for his son. One day the monkey ran away from the house and was discovered picking cotton right along side the black fieldhands.

The plantation owner headed back to the pet shop. "That monkey can pick cotton as good as a man. Give me a thousand of them."

"Sorry," said the pet shop owner. "I couldn't rightly do that!"

"Why the hell not?"

"Well, you put a thousand monkeys out there and before you know it they'll be movin' into our neighborhood. Pretty soon their kids'll be goin' to school and if you think I want one of their kids marryin' one of my kids, you're plum crazy!"

\*　　\*　　\*

## SOUTHERN POLACK

*A guy who thinks Black Muslim is a kind of cloth.*

\*　　\*　　\*

What do they call a Negro nuclear physicist in Alabama?
Nigger!

Andrews, a white Georgia farmer, hired Monroe, a Black to chop some wood. Monroe took the axe and began hacking away. But in a little while the farmer noticed Monroe sitting in the shade, watching another Negro do the work.

"Why you sittin' there doin' nothin' when I'm payin' you to cut that wood?" asked Andrews. "How come you got somebody else doin' it?"

"Ah hired him to do it for me," said Monroe.

"Is that a fact," said the white man. "How much are you payin' him?"

"Ah'm payin' him a dollar and a quarter," answered Monroe.

"Why would you want to do that?" snorted the white man. "I'm payin' you only a dollar!"

"I know," said the black, "but it's worth a quarter to be boss for once."

\* \* \*

Daniel Boone called his girl friend *Cumberland*. She had the biggest gap east of the Mississippi.

\* \* \*

## CRACKER JOCK

*A ball-bearing bag from Atlanta.*

A Negro civil-rights worker disappeared from a deep Southern town after bringing about registration of large numbers of Negroes. When he failed to show up, it was decided he had been killed and a search was begun.

Some days later the searchers located his body at the bottom of a river. Upon retrieving his body they noticed that he was tied and bound with chains and locks.

"Look at that damned nigger," said the Sheriff. "He tried to swim across the river with all them chains he stole from the hardware store."

\* \* \*

When the voting law came into effect, a young Negro girl entered the registration booth in Mobile.

"Ah wants to vote," she said.

"What party do you affiliate with?"

"Suh?"

"What party do you affiliate with?"

"Does Ah have to tell dat?"

"Of course."

"Den Ah'm goin' home and Ah ain't gonna vote. De very idea! De party Ah affiliates with ain't even divorced yet!"

Three cheers for sexy Dixie,
Her bed is not for sleep.
She has a lot of poontang,
But none she wants to keep.

*    *    *

Art Felkowitz, Miami Beach hotel magnate, mustered up this marvelous mood of merriment:

A couple of hillbillies from the backwoods country came into town to get married and brought their best man, Zeke, along. When they applied for a license, the clerk informed them that state law required blood tests before they could get a license, and told them there was a doctor around the corner who would make the tests.

As the M.D. took blood samples from the prospective bride and groom, Zeke watched with great interest. "What're you doin', Doc?" he asked.

"We check for venereal disease," said the physician. "If we find any, the wedding can't take place until it is cured."

"Well then," said the best man, "ain't you gonna test my blood?"

"What for?" asked the doctor. "You're not getting married, are you?"

"Oh, no," said Zeke, as he pointed to the couple, "but I'm gonna board with 'em!"

Ernie Mills, the Independent News ace regional sales supervisor, suggested this saga of silliness:

A New York book salesman, traveling through the South, asked a village store owner, "Have you seen our new volume, *The Problems of Incest?*"

"That's what I hate about you Yankees," the Southerner sneered. "You take a simple family custom and turn it into a social issue."

\* \* \*

## TENNESSEE BRIDE

*You can spot her easily. The pregnant girl in the white dress.*

\* \* \*

"Neighbor, did you borrow my hoe?"
"Mistah, ah didn't even know your wife was in the business."

\* \* \*

## SIGN IN A SAVANNAH OFFICE WASHROOM

*Don't Let Your Fanny Do You Out of a Job.*

Dr. Jay Fleischmann, Baltimore's brilliant young eye specialist, offers this *bon mot:*

The Ozark farmer's wife had a baby each year for the past twelve years in a row. He finally went to a doctor for some advice. "Here's a gross of rubbers," said the doctor. "Just read the instructions on the label."

A year later, the hillbilly brought his wife in, pregnant again. "Did you follow the instructions on the box?"

"Yep, Doc! Sure did! The only thing was I didn't have no organ so I put 'em on the piano!"

\*     \*     \*

There was a young lady from Wheeling
Who'd indulge any whim men were
    feeling
  She'd put out good, straight,
  Or she'd vary her gait,
She took in more suckers when kneeling.

\*     \*     \*

Jim Furbee, the West Virginia Remington Tire distributor, says there's a small town in his state that has had exactly the same population for the last fifty years. The census takers have just figured out why. Every time a baby is born, a fella leaves town.

# BLUE GRASS QUEER

*My Old Kentucky Homo*

\*       \*       \*

And if you've wondered how a mountain gal holds her mountain likker, she holds him by his *mountain-eers*.

\*       \*       \*

Miami lawyer Arthur Davis relates this hilarious hunk of hijinks:

Down in the mountain country they were trying a rape case. The victim was on the stand.

"Now, young lady," the prosecutor began, "please tell the court in your own words of your experience. First, can you identify the man?"

"That's the one," the girl pointed.

"And when did this attack occur?"

"As I remember, it was last June, July, and August."

\*       \*       \*

Then there was the farmer's daughter who was sent home from the county fair 'cause she couldn't keep her calves together.

"Junior!" shouted the Arkansas housewife, "where's your paw?"

"He's down in the barn juicin' the cows," replied the boy.

"Well, you take these milk buckets down there and tell him he'd better bring back some *milk!*"

\*     \*     \*

Into town on his regular Saturday visit came a lanky Tennessee mountaineer and his young wife. In the crook of his right arm nestled a week-old baby.

The dry-goods merchant, who had not seen the couple in a long while, welcomed them. "Come on in, folks, glad ta see ya! Well, now, is that yore young 'un, Clete?"

"Well, yeah," said the mountaineer, after thinking for a moment. "I reckon it's mine. Leastways, it wuz caught in my trap."

\*     \*     \*

## SHOTGUN MARRIAGE
*Troth or Consequences*

Domita came up from Alabama to visit her cousin Velma, in New York. The gals decided to have their pictures taken as a keepsake. They entered a portrait studio and the photographer had them pose in front of a backdrop.

He set up his tripod and then ducked his head under the black cloth to make the final preparations.

"Honeychile," said Domita to her northern cousin, "what's he doin' under dat dere black cloth?"

"Oh," replied Velma, "he's gettin' ready to focus!"

"Bofus???"

# OVERHEARD AT A TUSCALOOSA TRUCK STOP

*Waitress:* Y'all gotta be kiddin'. After I've been standin' on my feet all day?

*Trucker:* Honey, who's askin' you to do it standin' up!

\* \* \*

Times may change but Southern hospitality will always remain. A Carolina tobacco planter found his daughter making love to their Northern guest on the hallway floor.

"Clarabelle!" he shouted. "Where is yo' Southern hospitality? Arch yo' back and get the ge'naman's balls up off that cold marble flo'!"

\* \* \*

Everyone in South Carolina raves about Myrtle Beach, the friendly resort. The girls are all looking for husbands and the husbands are all looking for girls.

\* \* \*

## SOUTHERN SAGACITY

*Better to sleep with an old hen than pullet.*

"Ain't that Emmy Lou somethin'?"

"She sho' is! Only twenty-three, and already she's had seven husbands."

"Seven?"

"Yep. Three of her own and four of her friends'."

\*   \*   \*

## SONG OF THE SOUTH

*I'm Taking My Girl to Miami, and Then I'm Going to Tampa With Her.*

\*   \*   \*

Townsend and Mitchell, two young Atlanta engineers, were reminiscing about their college days. "I sure wish I could have gone to Georgia Tech," remarked Townsend.

"Oh, hell, you wouldn't have liked Tech too much," said Mitchell. "The only graduates they have are football players and whores."

"It just so happens my wife graduated from Georgia Tech," snapped Townsend.

"Really?" said Mitchell, realizing his faux pas. "Tell me, what position did she play?"

61

She called her husband "Double Arkansas" because of his two Little Rocks.

\* \* \*

Vic Sutton, Hollywood talent agent with William Cunningham and Associates, came up with this classic commercial:

The manufacturer of a nationally known tonic for people with "tired blood" received this testimonial from a little old lady who lived on a farm in Tennessee.

"Before takin' your tonic," wrote the woman, "I was too tired to hoe the fields or pick the cotton. But after only two bottles of your delicious mixture I've become the best cotton-pickin' hoer in the country."

\* \* \*

*Chicago gal:* Horny men are all alike.
*Atlanta gal:* Horny men are all ah like, too.

\* \* \*

"No," cried Clarabelle. "Ah'm not that kind of girl. Besides, the grass is wet, Mama said I shouldn't, and two bits ain't enough."

Bermuda Schwartz, director of public relations for the Mutual Broadcasting System, tells about the New York salesman who had been shot to death in a small Southern city. The incident took place on a bus. An inquest was held and a witness was asked to tell exactly what happened.

"I was on the bus and in the seat in front of me was this real nifty-looking gal. A fella sits next to her and starts a conversation. He told her he was on a business trip for his firm in New York. Then, as bold as can be, he offered her five dollars to come to his hotel room. She turned red with embarrassment and refused to answer him. Then he offered her ten dollars, then twenty.

"The girl jumped up and cried, 'Isn't there a gentleman in this bus?'

"Then that man over there pulled out a gun and shot him!"

The coroner looked at the accused and asked: "What do you have to say?"

"Well, suh, ah'm a Kaintucky cuhnel, and ah won't stand for any dam' Yankee comin' down heah and raisin' prices!'"

# THE WEST

A motion picture actor told his psychiatrists, "I'm attracted to men instead of women."

The shrink replied, "You've come to the right place, handsome . . ."

\*   \*   \*

A fellow driving his car on Hollywood Boulevard, with the top down, was wearing a bright red shirt, a blue polka dot tie, an emerald green plaid suit, and a lavender beret. A motorcycle cop stopped him and made him pull over to the side of the road.

"What's wrong, officer?" asked the boy. "I haven't violated any traffic laws!"

"Oh, I know you didn't," said the cop. "I just wanted to hear how you talk."

# CALIFORNIA HUSBAND

*One who nags his wife about the other man he could have married.*

\* \* \*

California caterer Bill Jones contributed this cutie:

If a white man driving a black Cadillac is accused of White Power—

And a black man driving a white Cadillac is accused of Black Power—

What is a Mexican driving a red Cadillac accused of?

Grand Theft Auto.

Unless he has a fur lining around the steering wheel, a plastic Jesus on the dashboard, and two Styrofoam dice hanging from the rear view mirror—

Then it's his!

\* \* \*

In old California, a popular makeout spot was located on a bank covered with weeds. Lovers who came there always returned to town with burrs all over their clothes. That is why they named the village "BURR BANK."

# OVERHEARD IN LOS ANGELES DRUGSTORE

"Are you a Hollywood Harlot, or just another Cali-fornicator?"

\* \* \*

In a Las Vegas casino, a change girl discovered the following sign hung on one of the slot machines: *In case of atomic attack hide under this crazy machine—It's never been hit yet.*

\* \* \*

Comedian Dave Barry, who entertains in the Nevada gaming capital several times a year, is an expert on that city. "Las Vegas has all kinds of gambling devices," says Dave. "Roulette tables, slot machines, wedding chapels."

\* \* \*

There was a young lady in Reno
Who lost all her dough playing Keno
    Then she started to play
    In the old female way
And now she owns the casino.

*The only city in America where people sit in their Cadillacs and count nickels.*

\* \* \*

Mort Solowitz, the television game show prize king, delivered this delightful dash of drollery:

It was late afternoon in a small Oklahoma town. Joe, the owner of the local beer parlor, was lazily polishing glassware when his friend Mickey came running in.

"Joe," he shouted, "get over to your house real quick. I just stopped off to see if you were home and I heard a stranger's voice in your bedroom. So I looked in the window and, gosh, I hate to tell you this, but your wife is in bed with another man."

"Is that so?" said Joe, matter of factly. "What does this guy look like?"

"Oh, he's tall and completely bald."

"And did he have a thick red mustache?" asked Joe.

"Right, right!" yelled Mickey.

"Did you notice if he had a gold front tooth?"

"Damn it, man, you're right!"

"Must be that jackass Dick Roberts," said Joe. "He'll screw anything!"

# GAY TULSAN

*Oklahomo*

\* \* \*

Dan Deutsch, president of the California Optical Fashion Center chain, cherishes this classic:

Every newspaper in Los Angeles had a reporter and photographer at the office of the prominent eye doctor. It seems the ophthalmologist had recently performed a successful sightsaving operation on the wife of the country's most celebrated painter.

The pop artist, in addition to paying the specialist his usual fee, had gratefully insisted on painting one wall of the doctor's waiting room. The subject of the mural was an immense, multicolored human eye, in the center of which stood a perfect miniature likeness of the good doctor himself.

While cameras clicked and most of the newsmen crowded around the famous artist for his comments, one cub reporter drew the eye doctor aside.

"What was your first reaction," he asked the M.D., "on seeing this fantastic human eye covering an entire wall of your office?"

"My first thought," reported the doctor, "was thank goodness I'm not a gynecologist!"

Jerry Svendsen, the energetic entertainment director in Sun City, Arizona, supplied this socko saga:

Retiree Amos Matson, age seventy-three, went to the doctor for a physical. After the examination he listened to the results.

"You're not as young as you used to be," said the physician, "you're going to have to slow down. You don't smoke or drink so that's out. How about giving up, say, half your sex life?"

"All right, doctor," agreed Matson. "But which half do you suggest I give up—the thinking or the talking?"

*　　*　　*

## MONTANA MELODY

*If you don't want your marriage*
*To end in divorce,*
*Forget that your first love,*
*Was hung like a horse.*

*　　*　　*

In a recent poll, fifteen percent of the Indians thought that the United States was right in getting out of Vietnam. Eighty-five percent thought they should also get out of America.

While covering his Western territory, a New York salesman decided to visit an Indian reservation. As he wandered about the salesman was approached by a beautiful Comanche maiden who offered herself for fifty dollars.

"That's a lot of money," he said. "Manhattan Island only cost twenty-four."

"That's true," she said, "but Manhattan Island just lies there."

71

In a little New Mexico town, a pretty young tourist overheard a virile Navajo saying "Chance" to every passing female. Finally, her curiosity got the best of her, so she walked up to him and said, "Hello." To which he answered, "Chance."

"I thought all Indians said 'How!'"

"I know how—just want chance," he replied.

* * *

A spinster schoolteacher on her summer vacation was visiting the reservation at Yosemite. She spotted a big brave standing against a tree and became very curious about his sex life.

"How does a great big man like you get satisfaction up here where there are no young squaws?" she asked.

The Indian stared at her unbelievingly and then said, "You see cow?"

"Yes, I see cow . . . you don't mean?"

"Yes," said the brave, "me make love to cow. Also, you see horse?"

"Yes," said the spinster, horrified. "I see horse."

"Me make love to horse."

"Oh, dear!" cried the distraught old maid.

"No," grunted the Indian sadly. "No make love to deer. Run too fast."

# PEEPEE TEEPEE

*Rest room on the reservation.*

\*     \*     \*

Many, many moons ago the great Apache chief Cochise was nearly ready to enter the happy hunting ground. He called for Geronimo and Fallen Rocks, the two strongest and most courageous braves in the tribe.

"Each of you must go and seek buffalo skins," said Cochise. "One who get most skins will be the new chief."

About a month later, Geronimo came back with two hundred pelts, but Fallen Rocks did not return. They searched for him diligently, but he was never found. Indians never give up hope. In fact, even now as you drive through the Old West, you will see signs saying: WATCH OUT FOR FALLEN ROCKS

\*     \*     \*

An Indian squaw was explaining the facts of life to her daughter. "Stork not bring papoose," she pointed out, "it come by beau and error."

73

Why do they call that Indian girl "Revere Ware?"

She's well-built, nicely rounded, and has a copper bottom.

*     *     *

The Indian agent on a South Dakota reservation reports that the Sioux squaws have been practicing a variation on suburban wife swapping. They call it "passing the buck."

*     *     *

An Indian maiden, a Sioux
As tempting as fresh honeydioux
    Likes to show off her knees
    As she strolls past teepees
And hear the braves holler, "Wioux, wioux!"

*     *     *

Then there was the Indian chief who installed electric lights in the tribal latrine, thus becoming the first Indian to ever wire a head for a reservation.

*     *     *

## SITTING PRETTY

*Sitting Bull's fag brother-in-law.*

74

Martin Phillips, the ebullient stock broker with Bache & Company, gets boffs with this beaut:

Every time the cowboy rode through the Indian village, he would wave at the aged chief. In response the old man would give him the finger, in the usual vertical manner. Then he would turn his hand so that the third digit stuck out horizontally.

After a few weeks, the cowboy could stand it no longer. He stopped his horse and said to the redskin, "I know what it means to get the finger straight up, but what does it mean when you turn it sideways?"

"I don't like your horse, either!" replied the chief.

*　　*　　*

Ed East, top man at Newsstand Distributors in Utah, tells this titillating tale to tired travelers:

A distinguished Bostonian, stopping off in Salt Lake City on his way to San Francisco, met a little Mormon girl. "I'm from Boston," he said to her. "I guess you do not know where Boston is?"

"Oh, yes I do," answered the little girl. "Our Sunday School has a missionary there."

A rangy cowpoke strolled into the Silver Dollar Saloon and stopped one of the pretty dancing girls.

"Are you the head whore here?" he asked.

"No sir," she replied. "Miss Kitty is the head whore. All I get is the shaft."

*　　*　　*

A cowpoke is a cagey guy
　　Who has a lot of fun.
He samples every pretty wench
　　And never Mrs. one.

*　　*　　*

Mrs. Smythe introduced her voluptuous young companion to the handsome cowboy who was to drive them from the railroad station to the dude ranch.

"Charlie," she said, "this is an Eastern acquaintance of mine, Miss Green."

He gave the pretty blonde a long appreciative look and then turned to Mrs. Smythe.

"Ma'am," smiled Charley, "I'd be right proud to make your acquaintance."

Dottie and Linda, two New York tenderfoots, were spending the first day of their vacation at a dude ranch. As they were passing the corral, a big bull bellowed loudly.

"What a big pair of lungs that bull has!" said Dottie.

"Yeah," said Linda, "and they're almost dragging the ground, too!"

*     *     *

Business at a combination dude ranch and resort hotel, the Westward Ho, had been very slow. Suddenly, after the owner hired a new black bus driver to meet all trains, business began booming.

"How do you do it?" he asked the driver, who had just moved up from the Deep South.

"Ah, really don't know," replied the man. "When dat train comes chuggin' in, all ah do is hollah, 'Free bus to de Westward Ho House' and they all come pilin' in."

*     *     *

Then there was the dude cowgirl who came home from the men's bunkhouse with a straddle sore.

Cliff owned a big ranch and it kept him so busy it interfered with his sex life. He had to work from sunup to sundown. Whenever he was out in the pasture with the cattle and got the urge he'd send one of his ranch hands to fetch his wife, Betty. By the time Betty raced from the ranch house to the pasture, which was a good distance away, she would be too tired to satisfy her husband's wishes. In the evening, Cliff would be too exhausted to do anything but have his supper and hit the sack.

After several months, Cliff got an idea. "When I leave the pasture, I'll ring the fire bell," he said to his wife. "That's the signal to meet me. That way, you won't have to rush and you won't be too tired when I join you up at the house."

Betty agreed and the next afternoon while feeding the horses in the corral she heard the fire bell tolling. Betty headed for the ranch house, got undressed, hopped into bed, and waited for her husband.

Minutes passed, then a half-hour, then an hour. Two hours later Cliff came running into the bedroom and saw Betty in bed.

"What the devil are you doing there?" he shouted. "The darn chicken coops are on fire!"

# RAWHIDE

*New western-style brassiere—it heads
them up and moves them out.*

\*   \*   \*

Lulu Zezas, the Wyoming oil and
cattle queen, tells about a ranch owner
who was always complaining that his
boots were too tight.

"Why don't you have them
stretched?" suggested Lulu.

"Nothin' doin'," replied the rancher.
"These boots are too tight and that's
the way they're goin' to stay. Every
morning I gotta get up and round up all
the cattle that busted out during the
night, and mend the fences they tear
down, and watch my ranch blowing
away in the dust, and then spend the
evening listening to my wife nag me
about moving to the city. When I get
ready for bed and pull these tight boots
off, that's the only real pleasure I get
all day."

\*   \*   \*

What's a bar stool?

That's what Davy Crockett used to
step on in the woods.

Riding across the hot Arizona desert on his pony, Buck came upon an attractive young woman, completely naked, tied to the ground by four stakes. The grimy cowpoke leaned forward in his saddle. "What's goin' on here, ma'am?" he inquired.

"Oh, thank heavens you've come," she gasped. "A terrible thing has happened. Mexican bandits stopped our car, knocked out my husband, tied me up like this and raped me. Then they rode off with my husband and left me here to die."

The cowboy got down off his horse and began taking off his pants. "Ma'am," said Buck, "I guess this just ain't your lucky day!"

Clark burst through the swinging doors of the Sidewinders Saloon and shouted: "All right! Who's the smart-aleck that painted my horse green?"

Silence.

"Show yourself," challenged the cowboy, "if you dare!"

Suddenly, a seven-foot-tall, rough-looking bad man got up from the poker table and rested his hands on his gun handles. "I did it!" he said. "What did you want to tell me?"

"I thought you'd like to know," said Clark, swallowing the lump in his throat, "that the first coat is dry!"

\* \* \*

"Why do you want a divorce from your cowboy?" asked the lawyer.

"'Cause he's got the fastest gun in the West."

\* \* \*

*Father:* Well, son, didja win the big State Spelling Contest?

*Son:* No, Pa, I didn't. I missed the very first word.

*Father:* Yuh did? What was the word?

*Son:* Posse.

*Father:* No wonder you missed it. You don't even know how to pronounce it.

Television comedy actor Dick Patterson passed along this poignant pleasantry:

Hank was riding the range, a-singing and a-humming. Suddenly his horse reared and stopped. In front of them was a huge snake. Hank drew his gun and was about to fire when the snake cried: "Don't shoot! If you spare my life, I have the power to grant you any three wishes you make!"

"Okay," said Hank, figuring he had nothing to lose. "My first wish is a handsome face like Paul Newman. Second I want a muscular body like Mohammad Ali. And my last wish is to be equipped like my horse here!"

"Granted!" said the snake. "When you wake up tomorrow you'll have all those things."

Next morning, Hank awoke and rushed to the mirror. Sure enough, he had a face like Paul Newman and to his delight he saw a pair of massive shoulders and arms like Mohammad Ali. Then, glancing down in great excitement he let out a blood-curdling howl. "My Gawd, I clean forgot!" he babbled. "Yesterday I was riding Nellie!"

*     *     *

## AND TEXAS

A Houston resident wanted the late Louis Armstrong to fly his thirty-piece orchestra down to his ranch. The price was right but the King of the Trumpet wanted to know how many guests would be at the party.

"Ain't no party," said the Texan. "My doorbell chimes is busted and I feel neighbors who visit me like to hear music when they ring."

*   *   *

A man from San Antonio died and went to Heaven. St. Peter greeted him at the gate and asked, "Where are you from?"

"Texas!" he replied.

"All right, come on in!" said St. Peter. "But you're not going to be satisfied."

A Texas teenager told his daddy he needed some oil for his hair. His father bought him Oklahoma.

*       *       *

A big chauffeur-driven limousine pulled up in front of the Plaza Hotel in New York. As soon as the car stopped, a footman got out and carried a fifteen-year-old boy into the lobby. The boy's parents then got out of the car.

A woman passerby who had witnessed the entire scene turned to the boy's mother and said, "What a pity that such a handsome boy shouldn't be able to walk."

"My dear," said the boy's mother, "we are one of the richest families in Texas; our son never *had* to learn to walk."

*       *       *

Yvonne Schwartz tells about the Beaumont land baron who was shocked to receive his check back marked "Insufficient Funds." He was about to call the bank when he saw the notation: "Ours—not yours."

Y'all hear about the Texan who wanted his son to learn how to spell, so he hired a college marching band to spell out words for him?

*   *   *

Two mothers met on the street in Dallas. "How is your son?" asked the first.

"Real good," replied the other mother. "He just opened his second office. He and his wife now have three cars. Two in help. A winter home and a summer house. Everything is marvelous. How is your daughter doin'?"

"What can I say?" answered the other woman. "She has so many maids, butlers, chauffeurs, I've lost count. She and her husband have a home in Paris, one in Palm Beach, and one right here. They just bought a townhouse in New York. It's easy for them to go wherever they feel like 'cause my son-in-law just got his own jet plane."

"That's amazing!" said the first woman. "What does your son-in-law do for a living?"

"He's a senior at Texas University!" said her friend.

86

Gladys Altshuler reports that in one Texas millionaire's home, the rugs are so thick that no one in the family has seen anyone below the neck for years.

\* \* \*

Did you hear about the poor boy from Fort Worth who inherited five million dollars and then proceeded to run it into a small fortune?

\* \* \*

The farmer from Wichita Falls was asked how he liked his new Rolls-Royce.

"Fine," he replied. "I especially like the glass partition between the front and the back seat."

"Why?" inquired his friend.

"It keeps the hogs where they belong."

\* \* \*

In Cleveland, a Texas oilman made a phone call and screamed his head off when the operator told him the charge was sixty cents.

"What!" he roared. "Back in Amarillo, I could talk to hell and back for sixty cents."

"Maybe so," replied the operator curtly. "But from Amarillo that would be a local call."

Socialite Rose Eber tells about the guide who was showing a big rancher from Amarillo the one and only Niagara Falls.

"I'll bet," said the guide, "you don't have anything like that in Texas!"

"Nope," said the cattleman, "I reckon we don't—but we got a plumber back home who could fix that leak in ten minutes!"

\*   \*   \*

## TEXAS PRAYER

*Oh, Lord, we thank Thee for the bounteous blessings bestowed upon our great state; and we beseech Thee to look with favor upon those places where Your feet have not yet trod.*

\*   \*   \*

In Texas everything but a Caddy is considered a foreign car. On one highway between Galveston and Corpus Christi stands a sign with this legend:
KEEP OUR HIGHWAYS CLEAN
NO CHEVROLETS, FORDS, OR
PLYMOUTHS ALLOWED

Laura Danieli, exec director of the exclusive Phoenix Executives Club, tells about the Texan visiting Arizona:

"Do you have one of those big ranches with thousands and thousands of acres?" the Texan was asked.

"Nope," he drawled. "As a matter of fact, I've only got fifteen acres."

"Fifteen acres! Why, your place is so small I bet it doesn't even have a name."

"That's right," smiled the Texan. "Most people just call it downtown Dallas."

\*     \*     \*

## FORMER LUBBOCK LADY'S LAMENT

*Carry me back to dear old Texas*
*That's where all the very best sex is!*

\*     \*     \*

A cattle baron told the judge he wanted an injunction to prevent his wife from committing adultery. "You mean," said the Judge, "you want a divorce!"

"Hell, no! I want an injunction!" shouted the rancher. "That woman is the best piece of ass in Texas."

# TEXAS

Where the men yell, "Remember the
   Alamo!"
And the women yell, "Remember the
   Alimony!"

*       *       *

Stan Fertman, midwest sales veep
for Shields Jewelry, was invited to
attend a banquet in Houston. The guest
of honor was a Rhode Islander named
Rogers. During the cocktail hour
Rogers got kidded about the size of his
tiny state compared with Texas. All
through dinner, he suffered the usual
crowing about the great state of Texas.
The toastmaster who introduced him
even mentioned how small Rhode Island
was.

Rogers got to his feet, thanked the
members for their hospitality, and then
told the following story:

A Galveston oil man died and went
to that great eternal resting place.
Upon arriving there, he was surprised
at how similar the terrain was to home.

"My goodness," he said to the nearest
person, "I never expected Heaven to be
so much like Texas."

"Mister," said the man, "I'm sorry
to inform you, but this isn't Heaven!"

A Bostonian visiting San Antonio asked a native, "What is that dilapidated-looking ruin over there?"

"That, suh, is the Alamo. In that building, suh, 136 immortal Texans held off an army of 15,000 of Santa Ana's regulars for four days."

"Oh?" said the tourist from Massachusetts. "And who was that man on horseback on that hill over there?"

"That, suh, is a statue of a Texas Ranger. He killed 52 Apaches singlehandedly and broke up 38 riots in his lifetime. Where you from, stranger?"

"I'm from Boston. We have our heroes there, too. Paul Revere, for instance."

"Paul Revere!" snorted the Texan. "You mean the fella that had to ride for help?"

\* \* \*

One kid from Texas got all the way to the national spelling bee finals and then lost the prize. He couldn't spell "small."

\* \* \*

## TEXAS

*Where men are men, and sheep are scared to death.*

While attending a Las Vegas show, a wealthy rancher from Waco developed a big yen for a little girl in the chorus. Being the strong, silent type, he sent one of his assistants to approach the girl.

He went backstage and in a few minutes she agreed to spend a long weekend in Acapulco with the rancher, but on three conditions: That he give her a mink wrap, that he deposit $1,000 in her bank account, and that he have eight inches.

Next night the go-between returned to the chorine's dressing room. "It's all agreed, miss," he told her. "Here's the wrap, here's the deposit slip—and the boss says that if you really insist, he'll see a doctor about doing something to get rid of those extra two inches."

This story may be apocryphal but those close to Clint Murchison, owner of the Dallas Cowboys, swear to its authenticity. Murchison, who prides himself on having every seat filled for Cowboy football games, looked up into Texas Stadium one Sunday afternoon and saw a vacant seat right on the fifty-yard line.

He rushed up and asked a little old lady sitting next to it if she knew why the seat was vacant.

"It's my husband's seat," said the lady.

"Why isn't he here?" asked the football tycoon.

"Because he's dead!" replied the woman.

"Then why didn't you give his ticket to one of his relatives?" asked the owner.

"I couldn't," replied the old lady. "They're all at his funeral!"

\*   \*   \*

An Austin oil millionaire had been so busy making money all his life he'd never had time to learn to read and write. One night he picked up a pretty blonde at a cocktail lounge and took her to a nearby hotel. He took the pen from

the clerk and signed the register with an X. Then, after a thoughtful glance at the girl, he carefully drew a circle around the X.

"I've had people sign their name with an X before," said the bewildered clerk, "but what's the circle for?"

"Shucks, sonny," said the oil magnate, "when a man checks into a strange hotel with a gal he's just met, y'all can't expect him to use his right name!"

\* \* \*

A team playing baseball in Dallas
Claimed the umpire was blind out of
    malice
  While the umpire had fits
  The team made eight hits
And a girl in the bleachers named Alice.

\* \* \*

Wearing two six-shooters on his hip, Tex walked up to a soda fountain and ordered a hot fudge sundae.

"Yes, sir," said the pretty counter girl. "Do you want your nuts crushed?"

"If you do," he said, reaching for his guns, "I'll shoot off both your tits!"

Hollywood actor Bob Ross tells about the dusty farmer who pulled his mule wagon up to the boardwalk of a small Texas town. A fancy gunslinger, dressed in black, watched the farmer as he headed for the saloon, then followed him in.

The farmer ordered a beer and the gunslinger asked for a double shot of whiskey. The farmer sipped his beer, the gunslinger downed his liquor and ordered another. The farmer finished his beer and was walking back to his mule wagon when suddenly the gunslinger appeared behind him.

"Hey, Sodbuster! Did you ever learn to dance?" he shouted and then emptied both his pistols in the ground at the farmer's feet.

The farmer just stood there looking the gunslinger dead in the eye. Then reaching into his wagon, he pulled out a double-barrel shotgun and aimed it at the gunslinger's gut.

"Did you ever kiss a mule's ass?" he asked.

"No, sir!" screamed the gunslinger, "but I've always wanted to!"

Danny Crystal, motion picture music coordinator, passed this one along:

A giant Texan wearing a ten-gallon hat and high boots walked into an Abilene men's room, passed up the urinals and sat down.

An Easterner just passing through stood there amazed. "Guess I've been fooled by you big tough Texans," he remarked. "Why did you squat?"

"I'm right glad you asked me that, podner," said the Texan. "You see, I had a hernia operation day before yesterday and my doctor told me not to lift anything heavy."

\* \* \*

Comedian J. C. Curtis came up with this cutie:

The lanky Lubbock ranch hand was still a virgin at twenty-one, and so on his first trip to the big city he visited a brothel. He soon found himself lying in bed with a pretty partner. Sensing the lad was inexperienced, the pro gently took his hand and placed it on the source of her income.

"Is this what you're looking for?" she whispered softly.

"Well, I don't rightly know, ma'am," murmured the cowboy. "I'm a stranger to these parts."

Joe Sigmond, the 7-11 Productions producer-publicist, provokes guffaws with this piece of pleasantry:

A large group of men were gathered in one corner of a New York bar. The Great Gambini, a nightclub mentalist, was amusing the group with his uncanny skill in identifying each man's nationality by the shape of his head.

"That's a lotta bull," roared a Texan in the group. "I think you're a fake."

"Sir," said the mentalist, "not only can I tell a man's national origin, but I can even tell what school he attended."

"Buncha crap," sneered the man from the Lone Star. "Lemme see."

"Very well," said Bambini. "Now this gentleman here, he's from Princeton. Am I right, sir?"

"Why, that's right!" he confirmed.

"I could tell by the cut of your clothes. Now this man over here, he's from Yale. Am I right, sir?"

"Yes!"

"I was able to tell by his manner of speech. Now this man here, he's from the University of Toronto. I can tell by the crest on his blazer."

Then turning to the Texan, he shouted: "Texas A and M! right?"

"Well, I'll be a . . . How'd ya tell?"

"I noticed the insignia on your class ring a few moments ago while you were picking your nose!"

A sissified student at Baylor
Had a new suit made by his tailor,
   All sequins and sheer,
   And printed on rear
Were the words that he loved "Hello,
    Sailor!"

\*     \*     \*

Two El Paso cattle punchers were standing on the bridge over the Rio Grande, urinating in the river.

"The water sure is cold," said the first man.

"And deep too!" said the second.

\*     \*     \*